¡Viva Mexico!

Text by Antonio Haas

Photographs by
Nicolas Sapieha,
Bob Schalkwijk,
Francesco Venturi and Horacio Hernandez

M. T. Train / Scala Books
New York

First published in the United States of America in 1998 by M.T. Train/Scala
Books, New York and by Monarca Ediciones, Librería Britànica, Mexico, D.F.

Packaged by Maria Teresa Train

Design by Our Designs, Inc., Nashville

Color Separation, Printing and Binding by Sfera, Milano, Italy

Distributed in the United States by Antique Collectors Club,
Wappingers' Falls, New York

Distributed in Latin America by Librería Britànica, Mexico, D.F.

ISBN 968-7607-19-X

To Nick,
in memory of his love for Mexico.

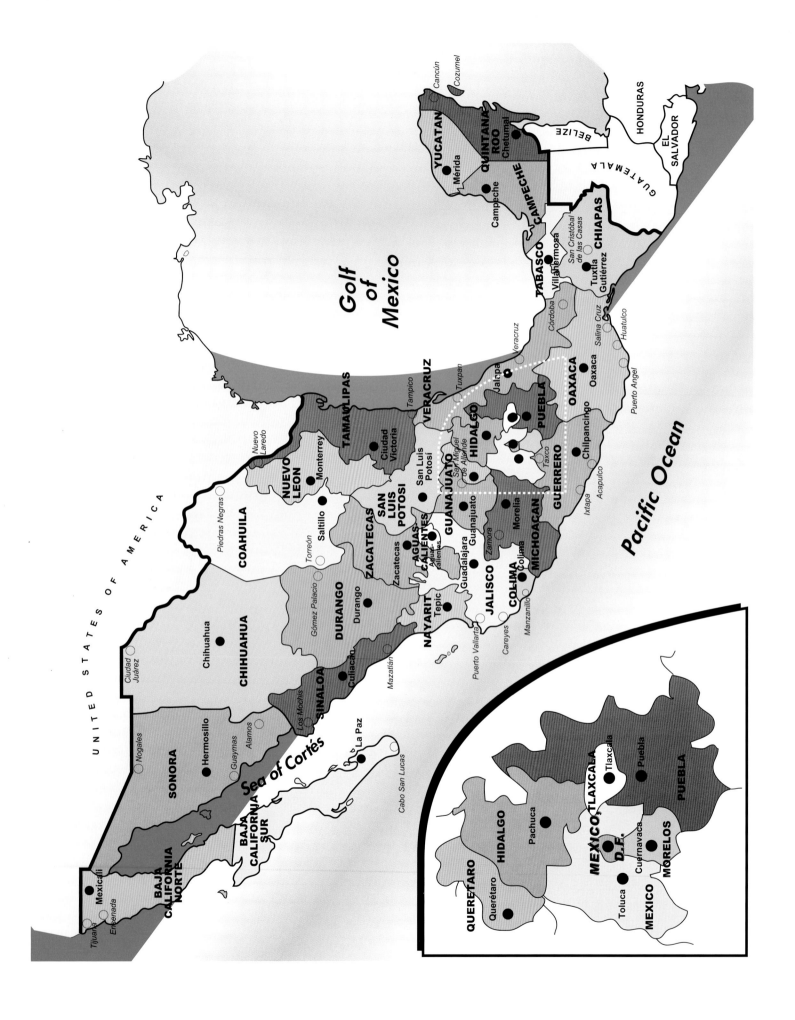

Table *of* Contents

Understanding Mexico

Diego Rivera, detail of "A Dream of a Sunday Afternoon in Alameda Park." Mural executed 1947-48 for the Hotel Del Prado and now housed in a specially-built pavilion near the Alameda Park at Balderas and Colon. Mexico City.

Understanding Mexico

The image most foreigners have of Mexico is like a sculpture by Henry Moore, strong and expressive but full of holes in vital places. It is the result of much tampering with the facts by political chroniclers who view history as an inexhaustible supply of modeling clay which they can shape to their own purposes.

The first big void that needs filling in spans most of our archeological past before the Aztecs. In that "dark backward abysm of time" there flourished opulent and various cultures whose names mean little or nothing to the nonspecialist today, so the word Aztec has become a generic term for everything pre-Hispanic.

After the fall of the Aztec capital in 1521 and the Spanish Conquest itself, there is another gap of centuries before the familiar 1860's tableau of that famous mano a mano between the Hapsburg Emperor Maximilian and Benito Juárez, the Zapotec Indian who defeated him, but who is seen by many foreigners as little more than a protégé of Lincoln. Yet this black hole in the general knowledge conceals the very centuries in which the Mexican nation developed its own particular character and began to play its historical role in the world.

After this Mexico blacks out for another fifty years until images of the 1910 Revolution light up the screen just long enough to convince our neighbors to the north that Mexico is a pit of desperados, swarming with generals and political assassins, though no sitting president has ever been assassinated here. Then history fades away once more, to be replaced by the silken beaches and glossy hotels of Cabos and Acapulco, Vallarta and Cancún.

The foregoing is not an idle simplification. It is, in fact, uncomfortably close to the truth. An astonishing number of well-read foreigners know little more than this about Mexico. The object of the present book, then, is to briefly reconstruct Mexican history and establish a certain continuity between these scattered episodes.

VISIONS AND REVISIONS

History is invariably written by the winner, and Mexico gets reinvented at least once after each major upheaval. In Aztec times, Itzcóatl burned the books to suit his needs, so the intent and extent of editorial revisions, including that of the Spaniards with respect to the Aztec codices, should not surprise us.

The War of Independence (1810–21), the Mexican-American War (1846–47), the anticlerical Reform laws and the Constitution of 1857 all produced radical switches in historical opinion. Maximilian's empire and the French intervention (1864–67) brought lasting discredit to the Conservatives who had tricked the guileless Archduke Emperor into believing that the Mexican people yearned for their old Austrian monarchs (an idea that probably did not sound as crazy then as it does now). After the liberal-republican defeat of the phantom empire, President Juárez returned to Mexico City and managed to re-elect himself one more time and to die in office in 1872. His successor, the liberal General Porfirio Díaz, ran for the presidency on a platform of no re-election and then proceeded to re-elect himself for seven consecutive terms. This time the conservative historians had a field day at the expense of the Liberal Party, though by the third re-election the older liberals had already become too conservative for the new generations.

Don Porfirio, however, managed to clear the countryside of its native bandits (frequently the survivors of defeated armies) while bringing in foreign experts to drag it reluctantly into the Industrial Age. He was fairly successful but he

Oil painting by Jose Muro Pico illustrating the ingenious Aztec farming system. Reed rafts, "chinampas," were covered in a thick layer of soil and floated on the lake.

did not measure the social and political cost, and his reign ended with the Revolution of 1910. Nevertheless, he was the only president who left more money in the till than was in it when he took over. Revolutionary historians are all too often rampant revisionists. They have deified Juárez at the expense of Díaz, whose colossal administrative achievements are to this day passionately ignored.

After Mexico's eleven-year struggle for independence, the United States emerged as our staunchest ally against Spain. The Mexican-American War, however, soon revealed the nature of this friendship. The loss of over half of Mexico's territory – Texas and everything between it and the Pacific coast, right up through California to Oregon– led to the general feeling that it was "the patriotic duty of every Mexican to consider the United States Mexico's worst enemy." Yet twenty years later, Juárez and his liberals, grateful for American aid against the French,

again looked on the United States as a loyal friend. After the Revolution, however, the villainous complicity of the American Ambassador, Henry Lane Wilson, in the assassination of President Madero, followed by the 1914 landings of the U.S. Marines in Tampico and Veracruz, definitely confirmed the United States as the official villain in Mexico's books.

Anti-*yanqui* feeling, however, has never stopped prosperous Mexicans from sending their offspring to American schools, their aches and pains to the Mayo Clinic (or, nowadays, Houston) and their savings to New York. Nor has it stopped the millions who cannot afford even the bare necessities of existence from taking the risk of crossing the United States border, in search of work and the kind of security unattainable in their native land. So, clearly, a large gap opens between the official view of the "Colossus of the North" and what the neediest of our people really think about it.

Our attitude toward Spain is also one of violent ambivalence. Spain is the country to which we owe our supreme cultural debt, our language. Yet we still seem to be fighting for our independence. We have never cut the umbilical cord. Spain has become the country Mexicans love to hate – after the United States, that is – and, also after the United States, the country we most like to visit.

In one of Diego Rivera's murals in the National Palace there is a list headed Mexico's "Contributions to the world" – maize, chocolate, avocadoes, tomatoes and chili peppers, among other things – which identifies the modern country with the pre-hispanic land. This is the official line. Aside from the fact that the list includes nothing man-made or of social significance, its supporters would do well to remember what Spain brought to us: draft animals, horses, cattle, wheat, citrus fruits, bananas, sugar cane, the wheel – not to mention wine, Christianity and the Spanish language. Even the Virgin of Guadalupe was imported from Spain (whereupon she presented herself miraculously to the Indian Juan Diego).

In the end we have to agree with the early Spaniards that the original natives were just not very practical. A workable wheel appears in some of their toys, for instance, yet it never occurred to them to give it real work to do. The Aztecs worshiped an image of Huitzilpochtli made of cornmeal paste – they had, in other words, an edible god before them – but instead of taking the further step of consuming him eucharistically, as the Christians did, they continued to allow him to eat them. Human sacrifice showed no sign of abating at the time of the Spaniards' arrival. Its overt purpose was to keep the celestial mechanics in working order, for the Indians believed that without an abundant supply of human blood the sun would be unable to rise the following morning.

Yellow opuntia cactus.

Mexico's attitude toward Hernán Cortés again reflects our ambivalence toward Spain. A Salamanca law school drop-out, he was beyond doubt the greatest of the conquistadors. In dealing with the natives he showed himself a matchless politician as well as a brave and crafty warrior: he was a settler and a lawgiver, not a hit-and-run exploiter. An advocate of Spanish-Indian intermarriage, his children were the first *Mestizos* (mixed blood, Spanish and Indian), who comprise the great majority of the Spanish-speaking Mexican people of today.

To many Mexicans, Cortés is still the one unquestionable hero of our history, the true founder of our nationality. Yet officially, especially since the Revolution, his name has been practically expunged from the records. There is no street or public monument dedicated to him in the country he so imaginatively helped create. Cuauhtémoc, on the other hand, the last of the Aztec emperors and Cortés's defeated foe, is the national hero. Such martyr-worship seems neurotic. Even his name, "Falling Eagle," symbolic of the setting sun, suggests defeat. Yet cities, towns and counties – even a brewery – are named after him, and his admirers gather once a year to celebrate his glory in Spanish, a language he abominated.

The Spanish Conquest has thus been turned into a politically correct Western. The Indians are the heroes, the conquistadors are the villains (with Moctezuma II in between, wandering about like Hamlet in the wrong play, half persuaded that Cortés was the returning Quetzalcóatl). Yet we know that many natives preferred the Spaniards to their Aztec overlords, so much so that they formed the bulk of Cortés's conquering troops, thus proving the truth of the aphorism that the conquest of Mexico was achieved by the Indians, and not the conquistadors, a fact frequently and deliberately overlooked.

We also know that the Aztec empire covered less than twenty percent of Mexico's present territory, yet the official premise is that anything Aztec is more authentically "Mexican" than anything contributed by the Spaniards, who created Mexico when they introduced the Aztecs and the other conquered tribes and territories to mainstream European culture.

The truth of the matter is that the Aztecs were Mexicas (mesh–chic–as), a particular group of Náhuatl–speaking Mesoamerican people– not Mexicans. This term evolved slowly and did not come into common use until well into the eighteenth century. We did not legally become Mexicans until after our break with Spain in 1810, with the creation of the first Mexican republic. As one of our writers put it: "*Yo soy mexicano, mexica, no!*"

Though we are neither Mexicas nor Spaniards, we are clearly heirs to both cultures, and some distinctive indigenous elements have survived alongside the Spanish in modern Mexican life and manners. Our diet, for example, is probably the one thing Cuauhtémoc would recognize: maize tortillas, chili peppers, a bounty of fruits and vegetables, some game and plenty of red meat (though not from any livestock he would have known). And the poorer, meatless diet of our Indian peasant probably differs little from that of his historical counterpart, the Aztec peasant.

Our vocabulary is another case in point. Mexican Spanish is so larded with words from the various vernaculars, especially Náhuatl, that several massive dictionaries of Mexicanisms have been compiled. In the Yucatán area, Mayan is still the lingua franca, and there are old gentlemen around who, having spent their school years in France, still count in French, argue in Spanish and lapse into Mayan about the house.

By the same token, the Spaniard strikes us as unnecessarily brusque both in his speech and his manner, from which it seems reasonable to assume that the peculiar Mexican circumspection, at once so mannerly and so noncommittal that it can be interpreted equally as timidity, deviousness, or simply the most exquisite courtesy, has come from our Indian roots.

Coral tree.

Certain institutions have survived in Mexico that were common to both Mesoamerica and feudal Spain. Of these, the most important is a system of common land tenure based on a right to the land and production, on usufruct rather than outright ownership, called the *ejido*. No understanding of twentieth–century Mexico is possible without a close look at that institution.

In the Aztec state, the communal lands were called *calpulalli*. Although they were inalienable, the right to farm them was individual and could be handed down from father to son. In Spain, the ejido was the village common, which in the walled towns lay immediately outside the exit gate. Hence the term *exido* (modern spelling ejido). The Mexican ejido, then, has clear antecedents on both sides of the family. It is more a revival than a survival, however, since all corporate land, including the Indian communities, was outlawed by the 1857 Constitution. In their attempt to liquidate and put into circulation the immense wealth held in mortmain by the church, the

Reform Laws turned the *comuneros* into small landowners. Unaccustomed to private ownership, they soon sold or mortgaged, and lost their land to the neighboring landowners, who thus built up their *haciendas* into vast estates while the Indians were reduced to hiring themselves out as *peons* on what used to be their own land. (Juárez's responsibility in the breakup of the Indian communities, incidentally, is seldom, if ever, mentioned). This tragic imbalance of property triggered the peasants' revolt led by Zapata, which in time became the mainstream of the 1910 Revolution and the raison d'être for the Agrarian Reform that defined the limits and conditions of farm land tenure. The mechanization of agriculture turned most of these limitations into obstacles. Bound to the land like feudal serfs, *ejidatarios* by the millions abandoned the land for the cities or illegally entered the U.S. The ruling party blithely sacrificed the ejidatario to preserve the ejido. The motive was neatly stated by a former Secretary of Agriculture: "The ejido has been organized to vote, not to produce." As the ultimate self-perpetuating voting machine, the ruling party could not afford to let it disappear. This process of agricultural suicide came to an end with President Salinas (1988–94) who had the Constitution amended to eliminate the ejido.

Our crushing centralism is another survival from our double-rooted past. It is the product of two absolute monarchies, the Spanish and the Aztec, merging into one under the equally centralist aegis of the Roman Catholic Church. In the nineteenth century, the decision of independent Mexico to finally turn itself into a Federal Republic had little practical effect: it did nothing to decentralize the country. Mexico, in sum, is the offshoot of two rich and powerful cultures which had in common numerous social and political institutions. Many of these have survived. The difference between the two empires, however, are even more numerous, and a brief look around shows that these, too, have continued into the present day.

Vestiges of Mesoamerica are all about us in Mexico, undigested and perhaps indigestible. The ruins of this civilization are what most travelers want to see when they visit Mexico. Though found on Mexican territory, they are correctly Mesoamerican, be they Olmec, Teotihuacán, Zapotec, Mayan, Toltec or Aztec. The surviving Indians are, however, indisputably Mexican. Millions still live in their cultural fastnesses, practicing their shamanistic cults with psychotropic drugs, such as the "god's flesh" mushroom of Oaxaca in the south and the peyote in the north. Some, like the Lacándones of Chiapas and the Seris of Baja, who once appeared to be doomed to extinction, are now thriving.

Of the city Indians, on the other hand, those who are not begging on the streets are lamentably *au courant* in both material and intellectual fashions. They are, in other words, exactly like their Creole and Mestizo counterparts. Nothing has replaced the ties that once bound them to their ancient dignities.

Oil painting of the Zócalo in Mexico City, 18th century.

Before Cortés

Tabasco. Olmec altar c. 1200 B.C. Royal throne with an Olmec noble beneath a jaguar pelt. The king wears a crown of leaves and flowers, and holds rope and dagger. Archaeological Garden of La Venta, Villahermosa. The garden was conceived by the Mexican poet, Carlos Pellicer.

THE OLMECS (1200–300 B.C.)

In order to fill in the pre–Aztec void, the colossal Olmec heads of Tabasco and southern Veracruz make a good starting point. Single blocks of basalt, each sculpted by masters, weighing as much as thirty tons, were found resting pensively on the soft alluvial floor of a rain forest, and in the soil of a swampy island, leagues away from the closest stone quarry. Without the wheel, how did they get there? Without iron tools, how did they come into being?

We know very little about the Olmecs. Even the name is a later Náhuatl designation, meaning "dweller of the rubber country." They did, however, create what is known as the mother culture of Mesoamerica, since it provided the basic crafts and techniques for all subsequent civilizations. It is now generally believed that it was the Olmecs, and not the Maya, who invented zero as a mathematical concept. Their culture dominated the period between 1200 and 300 B.C.. It was followed by the Classical period, which corresponds roughly to the first millennium of the Christian era, during which time three great cultures flowered simultaneously in Mesoamerica: the Maya in the Yucatán peninsula; the Monte Albán Zapotec in Oaxaca; and, in the high central plateau near what is now Mexico City, the culture associated with the sacred city of Teotihuacán.

Mexico City. Post-classic Mayan polychrome figure of the god Chac-mool, messenger of the gods. It was found in the shrine dedicated to the Aztec god Tlaloc in the Great Temple.

TEOTIHUACÁN (100–900 A.D.)

This greatest of pre-Hispanic city-states had a definitive influence on all later developments in Mexico. Its grandeur was unsurpassed. Giants were supposed to have built it, their huge buried bones filling everyone with astonishment (as well they might, since they belonged to extinct mammoths). Teotihuacán was the first true city to develop alongside a ceremonial center. At its height, with almost 200,000 inhabitants, it may well have been the most populous city in the world.

The Aztecs, coming upon its ruins, called it the City of the Gods, which is what Teotihuacán means (the root word *teo*, by a curious phonetic coincidence, meaning "god" in Náhuatl as well as in various Indo-European languages). Pilgrims came to worship there from the farthest corners of Mesoamerica, and took home its merchan-

dise, its crafts and styles. Moctezuma himself was said to make yearly pilgrimages to Teotihuacán. He was especially devoted to Quetzalcóatl, the Plumed Serpent, whose prediction of his own second coming so fatally weakened Moctezuma before Cortés.

Some time between 650 and 700, Teotihuacán was sacked and put to the torch by unknown invaders. It never recovered. The old population emigrated, founding new cities. Foreign peoples arrived and settled among the ruins. And following the twilight of Teotihuacán, the classic Maya and Monte Albán cultures also began to decay. The sack of Teotihuacán and the later plundering of Tula, the Toltec capital, show that native conquerors were every bit as destructive as the Spaniards were to be.

THE TOLTECS (900–1500 A.D.)

The southward migration of peoples never seemed to stop. Always pressing down from the north were the barbarous nomadic tribes known generically as *Chichimecas*, literally "sons of bitches."

Like all "new" tribes, the Toltecs came south from Chichimec country. They soon established themselves in the rich central valleys and made Culhuacan, near Xochimilco, their capital. They adopted the cult of the Plumed Serpent from Teotihuacán and in time passed it on to the Aztecs.

The name Quetzalcóatl, besides "Plumed Serpent" also means "precious or divine twin," quetzal feathers being considered precious, of

divine origin, while twin is a secondary meaning of *cóatl*, serpent. Among star-worshipers, the divine twin meant the planet Venus in its dual aspect as morning and evening star.

The worship of Quetzalcóatl was a key element in the development of the Toltecs. The Quetzalcóatl cult from Teotihuacán did not become a man-god legend until the appearance of the messiah-like Ce-Actl-Topiltzin, an inspired leader who lived around the year 1000 and assumed the deity's name. The historic Quetzalcóatl moved the Toltec capital north from Culhuacan to Tollan, later known as Tula, which became the seat of Toltec

Hidalgo. Giant statues of dead warriors, known as the Atlantes of Tula, whose duty was to follow the sun, stand atop the Morning Star pyramid in Tula. On their chests are stylized butterflies, the Toltec emblem. Tula was the ancient Toltec capital, founded at the beginning of the 10th century A.D., and destroyed by fire c. 1165.

power. This bringer of light left his followers but promised to return. And return he did. Some found him in the Spanish conquistador, others in the missionaries' Christ.

The mythical Quetzalcóatl that issued from the merging of man and deity was of supreme importance in pre-Hispanic lore. Historically, he was a civilizer, credited with the invention of writing and the development of the agricultural arts. He advocated the end of ritual wars and human sacrifice. His pacifism was his undoing. Priests of a bloodier cult ousted him and his followers, who migrated south to Cholula and eventually ended

up in Chichen Itza, at the time a modest Mayan outpost which they converted into the impressive city whose ruins we know.

Tradition has dealt kindly with Quetzalcóatl. It has metamorphosed him into a monotheistic messiah who stood firmly against human sacrifice. At the end of his life he is said to have built a raft and sailed off toward the eastern sky, promising to return on the year whose number he bore as his given name *Ce-Acat* (One-Reed). To Moctezuma's misfortune, this number coincided precisely with the year in which Cortés landed on the eastern shores of his empire.

The Mexica–Aztecs (1325–1521)

Mexico City. Replica of a Mayan temple or tomb crowned with many figures. National Museum of Anthropology.

The prestige of the Toltecs continued to grow even after the fall of Tula. Though the name, "place of rushes (*tules*)" was originally a metaphor for any populous city, when applied to Tollan it came to mean "city of peace and bliss," something like the New Jerusalem of Christian thought. The Toltecs were the great people of the past, and to be descended from them conferred instant aristocracy. The Mexicas grasped at once the significance of Toltec status, and as they rose to power, they sought legitimacy by marrying into the ruling family of Culhuacan. Even Moctezuma married a woman from Tula.

A pilgrim tribe from the Chichimec north, the Mexicas had come south many years earlier in search of their promised land, which would be marked for them by a cactus on which they would see an eagle devouring a serpent (a curious mythographic separation of the Plumed Serpent into its component bird and reptile elements). The sign appeared on a rocky island in the middle of the (then enormous) Lake Texcoco, and there they founded the city they called Tenochtitlán, "place of the wild prickly pear."

Eventually Tenochtitlán became the capital of the largest empire Mesoamerica would ever know.

Mexico City. Santa Cecilia, Acatitlán. Aztec temple dedicated to Tlaloc and the sun god. Post-Classic period.

Mexico City. The beheaded and dismembered Aztec moon goddess Coyolxauhqui, "She of the snake rattles on her cheeks." Museum of the Great Temple.

By that time, waging war with their neighbors had become the Aztecs' way of life. They fought not only for loot and tribute but also to satisfy their gods' increasing demand for human blood. This made them hugely unpopular overlords, so when Cortés arrived, the subject peoples were ready to pull away and the independent lords were only too willing to help the challenger.

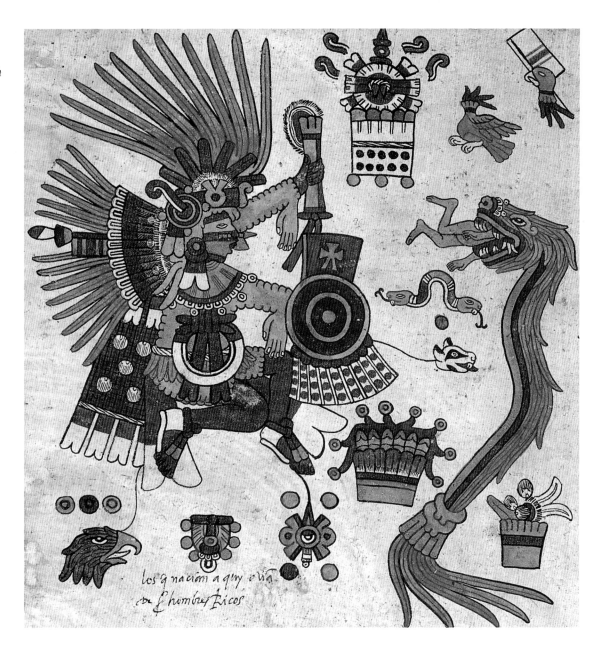

Aztec manuscript (Codex Borbonicus) from Tonalamatl. The figure center-left is the god Tezcatlipoca, the feathered serpent devouring a man is the god Quetzalcóatl.

First plate of the Mendocino Codex, showing the original layout of Mexico-Tenochtitlán. In the center is the figure of the Aztec tutelary god Huitzlopachtli in the form of an eagle.

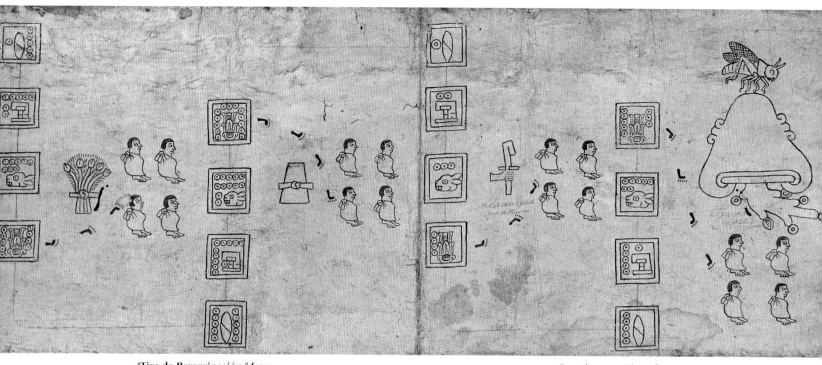

"Tira de Peregrinación," from
a Nahuatl codex, showing the
arrival in Mexico-Tenochtitlán
of people from Aztlán.

Opposite page: View of
the aqueduct which the
natives are building
from Chapultepec to
Mexico-Tenochtitlán.

Aztec funeral rites.
Aztec manuscript
(Codex Magliobechiano).

Human sacrifice.
Aztec manuscript
(Codex Magliobechiano).

First meeting of Cortés and the Emperor Moctezuma on the Iztapalapa causeway, November 8, 1519. 18th century Italian engraving.

THE CONQUEST

Cortés was always lucky in his timing. He dropped out of Salamanca in time to take part in the conquest of Cuba. Placed in charge of an expedition to the Mexican mainland, and correctly suspecting a plot to replace him, he shipped out before the appointed time. Once on shore and still feeling threatened, he summoned his officers and created the municipality of Veracruz just in time to put himself legally beyond the reach of his enraged superior. And – an unexpected bonus – he landed in 1519, which in the Aztec calendar was *Ce Acatl*, the very year in which the mythic Quetzalcóatl had promised to return.

The news of Cortés's landing burst on the Aztec court like a nova. Who else could this be but the departed god come to reclaim his heritage? Moctezuma sent gifts of gold, turquoise and quetzal feathers, and a polite message to the effect that the Emperor was not "at home."

Gold rooted the Spaniards to the new land. Cortés, correctly reading the mood of the natives, exploited their hostility toward the Aztecs and pressed the Spanish emperor's claim right up to Moctezuma's throne. After Moctezuma's death and Cortés's temporary defeat by Cuauhtémoc, the independent city-state of Tlaxcala gave Cortés asylum and helped him to restore his forces. Without the support of the Tlaxcaltecas and about forty thousand other natives, Cortés and his straggling body of Spaniards could never have taken Tenochtitlán, which confirms the fact that the conquest was effected by the Indians, not the Spaniards.

The city fell on 13 August, 1521. It took Cortés a scant two years to carry out what is known as the Conquest of Mexico.

That unfortunate phrase, "the Conquest of Mexico," has been responsible for much of our traditional resentment of Spain. That Mexico, after all, was not our Mexico. "We" Mexicans were not conquered: the Aztecs were. And the conquered land was not Mexico, but the Aztec Empire, which became the Viceroyalty of New Spain. Yet the feeling persists, after centuries of rancor and misunderstanding .

The Spaniards wanted gold and they did not hide the fact. After one look at Moctezuma's gifts nothing could have held them back." My companions and I suffer from a disease of the heart which can only be cured by gold," said Cortés to Moctezuma's ambassadors, by way of excusing his refusal to leave the land.

Not surprisingly, then, the quest for gold was the initial force behind the colonization of New Spain, which was undertaken as a joint venture by the Crown, Cortés and other enterprising officers. As soon as they got their bearings, the conquistadors found there was a distinct division between the settled, civilized, agricultural south, the main source of the Aztec empire's wealth, and the barren, mountainous wilderness to the north, the country of the savage, nomadic Chichimecs. So the conquistadors' first step was to take over the rich agricultural south. This they did by means of a legal trust, the *encomienda*, whereby the population of whole villages and towns, or even regions, was farmed out to the Spaniards to be educated and christened in exchange for personal services. This encomienda fulfilled the Spanish Crown's agreement with Rome, by which Spain could only legitimately own the land if it undertook to convert the conquered natives and instruct them in the Christian faith.

The conquistadors-turned-trustees, *encomenderos*, cared nothing about their charges' souls (with the notable exception of Cortés himself). They had, after all, undertaken the conquest at their own expense, and considered the encomienda

Mexico City. Silver and gold cross, 16th century. Franz Mayer Museum.

quite simply their due, so they proceeded to squeeze it for all it was worth, making it, in practice, indistinguishable from slavery.

As the wealth of the Aztecs was funneled into the treasure chests of Spain, the landscape changed, though not the lot of the native inhabitants. Instead of pyramids, tombs, and temples rising from the forest, bell towers, churches and monasteries now appeared in the new settlements. In both cases the building was done by Indian slave labor, but now at least they had iron tools and wheeled contraptions. The earliest convents functioned as schools, farms, hospitals and orphanages, and the mendicant orders that built them were the Indians' principal advocates before the Crown .

The missionaries abominated the encomienda. They agitated violently in support of the Indians, even taking their cause to the Council of the Indies, and to the King himself. The Crown even-

Mexico City. A striking example of the Flowered or Crowned Nuns, a genre peculiar to Mexico. National Museum of the Viceroyalty.

tually paid heed and promulgated the New Laws of 1542, legally abolishing the encomienda. Despite the howl set up by the encomenderos, the Crown slowly but surely deprived them of all their de facto privileges. A royal decree of 1591 declared all land in New Spain to be Crown property. They could however, purchase the land from the Crown if they wished to obtain clear title. After 1615, all lands lacking proper title were auctioned off. By 1648, most properties had been legalized and the ex-encomendero or his descendants could take full possession of their lands. These properties became the first haciendas.

Land, however, was practically worthless without the Indians' free labor, so the landowners devised a means of nailing down the native population. Playing on the Indians' innocence in money matters, the *hacendado* extended credit to his peons in the hacienda's commissary – the *tienda de raya* – far beyond the peon's ability to pay. Since he could not legally leave his employer while owing him money, this practice inevitably resulted in a system of serfdom through debt. Such debts were passed on from father to son. Eventually, the peon and his family became part of the hacienda's inventory and their debt was included in the purchase price of the hacienda.

In the meantime, the search for precious metals continued, and was in time richly rewarded, though not so much by gold as by the silver strikes in the badlands to the north. Prospectors braved the Chichimecs to reach their Eldorado and stake out their claims. Settlements appeared around every new mine. Merchants followed in droves and soon became bankers to the local populace of farmers and prospectors. Fortunes were made and lost overnight and once prosperous communities became ghost towns in the general vicinity of the great mining centers. Trade routes opened between the mines and Mexico City. At first, provisions and draft animals were still so prohibitively expensive that cattle ranches and produce farms were soon established near the mines. The Crown built roads and garrison towns, *presidios*, to protect the bullion it so desperately needed. Troops were sent to clear the land of Chichimecs, who in a single generation had become superb horsemen. Then the original conquistadors, Cortés included, were shunted aside by the viceroys and the lawyers, establishing in time the absolute power of the Crown. Three centuries later its profoundly weakening effects began to show. In the absence of incentives, no new race of conquistadors emerged to take the northern marches by brute force. For a long time the north remained almost as sparsely settled as when it had been exclusively Chichimec land, its frontiers no more than a judicial and cartographic convention. Early in the nineteenth century, pioneers from the United States started going west in considerable numbers. Many settled in Mexican territories. By the 1830's, they outnumbered the Mexicans in Texas and in much of California, and that situation eventually led to the loss of Texas and its incorporation to the United States.

Modern toys are offered to Baby Jesus in this shrine.

27

Whatever the faults of the Spanish Crown, it never neglected its missionary obligations. "The spiritual conquest of Mexico" is a chapter of grace and glory. Cortés's mercenarian chaplain, Bartolomé de Olmedo, a saintly and prudent man, always tried to temper the conquistadors' zeal for the shorn Indian lamb.

When the twelve Franciscan "apostles" arrived in 1524, Cortés astonished the natives by kneeling to kiss the hem of the friars' tattered habits. They asked if the newcomers were "like Father Bartolomé." Once reassured, they willingly accepted definitive conversion.

This took place not so much by discarding past beliefs as by the addition of new ones and the adaptation of the old. Syncretism is the term for the process, and neither the Church nor the natives were new at the game. The Aztecs had picked up many a belief in their wanderings, most notably the cult of the Plumed Serpent. Christianity simply added another layer of beliefs to their religious baggage – one, moreover, which proved remarkably easy to carry.

Certain theological concepts stumped them, however, especially those unsupported by pragmatic results. The Eucharist, for example. The idea of eating God's flesh instead of vice versa certainly provided a welcome change from Aztec practice, though it could hardly have been new to Indians who ritually ate the hallucinogenic mushroom known precisely as "god's flesh": *teonáncatl*. But eating the mushroom actually produced a rush of divine power through the bloodstream, whereas the communion wafer seemed to be totally ineffective. Prudent Indians continued both practices just in case.

Woodcut representing the apparition of Our Lady of Guadalupe, who revealed herself to a poor Indian named Juan Diego in 1531.

The natives took readily to the ritualistic rather than doctrinal approach, and there the Church's genius for syncretism won the day. The missionaries had themselves been converted by their love for the Indians, for their languages and civilization, a love of their virtue and of their weaknesses which frequently led to their turning against the conquistadors in defense of the Indians. Armed with their knowledge and practicing their own brand of syncretism, the missionaries allowed their converts to preserve many of their religious practices, eliminating only human sacrifices and the gods who demanded them. Any native deity that could be fitted into the Christian pantheon soon found his niche there. Presently, a sanctuary to the dark-skinned Virgin of Guadalupe rose on the hilltop where the Indians had previously worshiped Tonantzin, their revered mother-goddess. This was the Church's greatest tactical triumph in Mexico. It both encouraged the early converts' adoration of their native deity and satisfied the Spaniards' nostalgic devotion to their own Virgin of Guadalupe in Extremadura.

The Virgin of Guadalupe is the essence of the spirit of Mexico. This is no exaggeration. During the War of Independence she was the patroness of the insurgents. Now even atheists are devotees. The painter Diego Rivera, an outspoken, hardcore Communist, said she was "the sole symbol of our national unity. There is no other in heaven or earth." A Mexican may disbelieve in God, but never in *La Virgencita de Guadalupe*, Tontantzin-Our-Revered Mother.

Opposite page: Mexico City. The richly-carved Churigueresque façade of the 17th century in the sanctuary annexed to the Metropolitan Cathedral.

Napoleon's seizure of the Spanish throne left Mexico without a legitimate monarch, and the Mexicans opted violently for independence. Mexico's War of Independence began in 1810, but independence was not fully achieved until 1821. At that time, Mexican conservatives, pure-blooded Spaniards to a man, seeing Spain adopt the liberal Cádiz Constitution, joined forces with the insurgent leaders and severed Mexico's ties with the home country. Thus history runs full circle: just as the Indians had helped to achieve the conquest of Mexico, the Spaniards were later the prime movers in establishing Mexico's independence from Spain.

Spain's withdrawal from Mexico in 1821 left a power vacuum as obvious as that which had followed the collapse of the Classical civilization a thousand years earlier. Now, however, there were no strong, militaristic Chichimecs or Mixtecs to step in and take over. Mexico was splintered into irreconcilable factions during most of the nineteenth century; centralists fought federalists, conservatives fought liberals, Republicans fought Imperialists, even Yorkist and Scottish-rite Freemasons struggled for power. That, of course, is what makes democracy work. Not in Mexico, though. Here it produced an endless civil war. Finally two men appeared who were strong enough to put a stop to it, strong enough to grasp power and use it to impose order on the prevailing chaos. Both were natives of Oaxaca: Benito Juárez and Porfirio Díaz.

Benito Juárez (1806–1872) was a pure-blooded Zapotec Indian who did not learn to speak Spanish until he was thirteen years old. Destined for the priesthood, he became a lawyer instead, a professor of law and governor of Oaxaca. After that he occupied some of the highest federal posts during the stormy decade of the 1850's which ended with the Three Years' War. In 1858 Mexico found itself without a head of state, and Juárez, as President of the Supreme Court, legally succeeded to the presidency.

A series of financial and military crises followed the Three Years' War culminating in the French Intervention and the Second Empire. Taking advantage of the general discord, the Catholic conservatives in 1863 offered the nonexistent imperial throne of Mexico to Maximilian, who turned out to be as liberal as Juárez, with the result that the Papal Nuncio left the country in a towering rage. The country then split into Imperialist and Republican factions and Juárez was on the run most of the time. The quarreling factions buried the hatchet just long enough to get an army together in support of Juárez and the Republic. In 1867, the defeated Emperor Maximilian was shot by a firing squad outside Querétaro. His last words were *"Viva Mexico!"*

Meanwhile, Porfirio Díaz (1830–1915), a pupil and protégé of Juárez in Oaxaca, had joined the army and risen to the rank of Brigadier General. When the French left Maximilian to his fate, Porfirio Díaz mopped up the remaining Imperialist detachments in the south, and ending up in Mexico City, which he turned over, together with his army's funds, to the Juárez government.

The parting of the ways came with Juárez's re-election in 1870, after he had already been twelve years in the presidency. Díaz rebelled against his old friend and mentor with the slogan "No Re-election!" Ironically, the Revolution, which after thirty years tumbled Díaz from power, was sparked with the very same slogan.

The social and political divisions have been so deep among Mexicans that even the American annexation of over half our territory did not produce a uniform reaction among Mexicans. Nor did it prevent Juárez himself and the government of the restored republic from being fervent admirers of the colossus of the North. To this day there are Mexicans who, outraged by government corruption, are likely to rhetorically ask "why did the Americans stop at the border?" The answer, of course, is that they didn't. In 1847 American

Opposite page: Puebla. The Cathedra in Cholula. The city was once reputed to have 365 churches, one for each day of the year. It was the site of the definitive battle before the Spaniards reached the Aztec capital.

Mexico City. Emperor Maximilian.
Oil on canvas by Albert Graefle,
Munich, 1865. Chapultepec Castle.

troops took Mexico City with very little trouble, mainly because the various political factions were too busy squabbling among themselves to defend their country, and they preferred the foreign invasion to the triumph of their political rivals.

Mexico, it should be clear by now, is such a bag of contradictions that even the most thoughtful find it difficult to understand. The Revolution of 1910, which we proudly and correctly call the first social revolution of the century (thereby putting the Russian uprising of 1917 firmly in its place), did not end with Don Porfirio's defeat and exile. The shooting and killing and brush-fire rebellions went on until 1929, when the ex-president and strongman Plutarco Elías Calles put a stop to it by uniting the two- hundred-odd warring factions under a single political umbrella. The party he created is still in power. It is now called the PRI, an acronym for *Partido Revolucionario Institutional*, a fantasy title which implies that it is possible to be both revolutionary and institutional at the same time .

By 1982, Mexico was in a state of economic chaos brought on by the irresponsible policies of Presidents Alvarez Echeverria (1970–76) and López Portillo (1976–82). Between the two of them, they increased the foreign debt from a manageable 4.5 billion U.S. dollars to an impossible 80 billion dollars. The domestic debt was considerably larger, and the commercial interest rate had gone from 12 percent a year to 150 percent and more.

As a believer in big government, Echeverria had declared war on both industrial and agricultural entrepreneurs, nationalizing many of the biggest enterprises and decreeing the expropriation of legally immune farmland. To manage his enormous and mostly utopian projects (of which only the tourist mecca of Cancún survived) he created hundreds of thousands of bureaucratic jobs every year, and did not stop until the country ran out of money. Previously, our paper currency had been printed by the American Banknote Company. Now Echeverria bought his own printing press and, thinking he could print himself out of his corner, he started to print his own money by the

Mexico City. The elegant oval patio of the Buenavista Palace, now the San Carlos Museum, was designed in the neoclassical style by Manuel Tolsà for the Marques de Sierra Nevada. It is known for its semi-elliptical style. Begun in 1803.

33

Mexico City. David Alfaro Siqueiros, detail from "The Dictatorship of Porfirio Diáz to the Revolution" representing Diáz crushing the constitution underfoot and entertaining his supporters with dancing girls. Chapultepec Castle.

truckload. The result was an unbridled race between inflation and the commercial interest rates.

Since López Portillo did little to control the spending or to reduce the bureaucracy, investment capital – both foreign and domestic, public and private – fled the country like the plague. Finding no way to staunch the hemorrhage, concurrently with his last annual presidential report, Portillo nationalized the banking system and artificially pegged the price of dollars held in bank accounts at half their market value.

The problem was political, and crystal clear: the unbounded paralegal powers of the presidency, which had, in effect, canceled all the checks and balances embodied in our democratic Constitution. Owing to the hundreds of presidential amendments, the president now had unchecked power to do anything he wished with the economy and the political orientation of the country, including the power to handpick every state governor, and his own successor as President. The parties of the opposition were held to a strict minority in all federal elections (a government agency counted the votes). Their only use was as window dressing in Congress.

The situation bottomed out after President Carlos Salinas (1988–94) left office. This finally made people sit up and take notice. The country had touched bottom from both the economic and the political point of view. The PRI was losing members in droves, among them some of the oldest and most respectable figures.

In its present state, Mexico is a recovering alcoholic. The angst is there, and the tragic mix of extreme poverty and overpopulation has created a climate of violence that may require the equally extreme measures of a country at war with itself. With regard to the economy, however, it is definitely daylight at the end of the tunnel. Government overspending has been brought painfully to a halt. In the federal elections of July 6, 1997, the opposition parties won a majority in the lower House, as well as the governorship of the recently created state of Anahuac, also known as Mexico City.

Mexico is still a long way from recovering the situation we had when Echeverria took office, but for the time being, at least, we are headed in the right direction. The Old King was right: in nations as in individuals, "ripeness is all."

Teacapán, Sinaloa
November 1998

Mexico City.
Diego Rivera,
"The Great City
of Tenochtitlán."
Mural in the
National Palace,
1945.

Mexico City.
Diego Rivera, "Wall
Street Banquet."
Among those
reading the ticker
tape are John D.
Rockefeller,
Henry Ford and
J.P.Morgan. Part
of the mural
commissioned
by the Ministry
of Education, 1925.

35

CHAPTER 1

Mexico City

(Future State
of Anahauc)

Tenochtitlán on the lake of Texcoco
when Cortés arrived in 1519.

The Angel of
Independence, by
Rivas Mercado.
Mexico City's best-
loved statue was
commissioned for
the Independence
Centennial, 1910.
The angel towers
above the Paseo de
la Reforma and has
become an emblem
of Mexico City.

Mexico City

FUTURE STATE OF ANAHUAC

The very heart of Mexico City is the vast civic space of the Zócalo, traditionally the site of the island where the Aztecs first saw the eagle devouring the serpent on top of a prickly pear. This symbol can be seen on the Mexican flag that flies every day from the flagpole in the center of that huge square. In the northwest corner are the excavated ruins of the Great Temple of Tenochtitlán, solidly flanked by the cathedral and the National Palace – Church and State, heart and head of the Mexican people – sitting kitty-cornered from one another in massive though precarious equilibrium. The cathedral bears firmly down on the Sacred Precinct of the Aztecs, part of which was incorporated into its foundations in a sort of architectural syncretism, where it can be seen by anyone with access to the underground passageways near the spot where the great Temple of Tenochtitlán once stood. The National Palace rises from the foundations of the palace of Moctezuma himself. There is no doubt who won the war.

A few blocks to the north there is a curiously quiet spot, a bell of silence in the midst of the torrential traffic and the teeming apartment blocks of modern Tlatelolco, once the twin capital of Tenochtitlán. This too is a ceremonial spot, a square of sunken turf bounded by the steps of an Aztec temple demolished in 1521 by the soldiers of Cortés during the final battle of the conquest. Beside it stands the primitive Franciscan church of Santiago Tlatelolco, another visible reminder of the triumph of Spanish arms and the Christian faith. To the south, beyond a

Plaza de las Tres Culturas blends pre-Hispanic, colonial and contemporary buildings. A pyramid in the foreground and the Church of Santiago behind.

View of the Cathedral. Oil painting by Carlos Paris, c. 1834. The Cathedral took over three centuries to build, starting in 1525. The dominant styles of most Mexican architectural periods are represented in this impressive religious monument.

strip of lawn that makes symbolic room for the intervening centuries, there rises the black-and-white, glass-and-marble tower that houses the Secretariat of Foreign Relations, our connection with the modern world. This place is called the *Plaza de las Tres Culturas*. An inscription on a marble plaque informs us that, "On the 13th of August of 1521, heroically defended by Cuauhtémoc, Tlatelolco was taken by Cortés. It was neither a triumph nor a defeat, but the painful birth of the Mestizo people that are the Mexicans of today."

A fine sentiment, elegantly expressed and dialectically impeccable: thesis, Aztec culture; antithesis, Spanish Christianity; synthesis, modern Mexico. Unfortunately, it does not quite correspond to the facts. A satisfactory and stable synthesis has yet to be achieved. Mexico remains a house divided, a triptych of living cultures that coexist in time and place, though too often with little or no mutual contact or understanding. The "painful birth" is a work in progress: Mexico is still in labor. In Mexico, the word "Mexico" may refer to three different things: the country, the state or the city. To avoid confusion we will abide by the following rules. "Mexico" alone will refer to the entire country; "State of Mexico" refers to the federal entity, and Mexico City (or "D.F.") will refer exclusively to the capital city.

Buttresses and cupolas of the Cathedral.

Unless the smokestack industries are banished from the valley and the federal government is moved far enough away to place it out of the reach of commuters, Mexico City is doomed. This is the dismal truth. The incomparable mountain valley of Mexico, Tenochtitlán, which Alfonso Reyes once called "the air's most limpid domain," is now the biggest bowl of smog in the world. The facts alone are frightening. The valley of Mexico contains the D.F. plus twelve industrial municipalities pertaining to the neighboring State of Mexico .

The valley area, with a mere 0.005% of the national territory, lodges close to 20 million inhabitants – 20% of Mexico's total population; and 50% of the country's industrial capacity is located there.

Mexico can barely hold its head up now. It has become an octopus, every arm busily scavenging and feeding the insatiable capital city, which swallows up everything with scant respect for our federalism and our sporadic attempts at grassroots democracy. Since the federal election of 1997, the states and the provincial cities of the industrial north have been fighting back. As both the ceremonial center and the administrative plexus of the republic, the city is always packed with petitioners, especially in the government offices. The religious center of Mexico is also there – not in the cathedral, as one might think, but in the shrine of the Virgin of Guadalupe. This is the magnetic pole for all true Mexicans,

Opposite page: Full view of the Altar del Perdon in the Cathedral.

Detail of Altar del Perdon, with a portrait of St. Philip.

including Marxists and practicing atheists. Every year on 12 December, the anniversary of the Virgin's apparition in 1531, pilgrims troop in from every part of the country, some advancing on their knees and wearing scapulars of spiny cactus leaves. The whole city comes to a standstill.

The failure of the agrarian reform has poured millions of peasants into the valley area, where misery at least has company, and even the unemployed have a sporting chance of somehow getting along. About 5 million of the 17 million inhabitants live at a bare subsistence level. Their squalid shanty towns in sand pits, or cheek–by–jowl with some of the more August residential districts, are a vivid reproach to the system. Take the "Marías," those tiny Indian women who come down to the city from their native mountains rarely knowing more than a couple of words of Spanish. They sit on the sidewalks of the *Zona Rosa* (the pink–light district, with everything that implies). Many simply beg, though the more enterprising sell black avocados, peanuts or rape root (*jicama*). They tread the same pathways toward Tenochitlán and speak the same language as their Otomí forebears.

For bright, ambitious youngsters from the provinces, with no private means to sustain them, Mexico City has traditionally been the only option. An internal drain toward the capital has existed since the earliest days of the republic, which led a famous female wit of the time to say "outside Mexico City, it's all Cuautitlan" – the sticks. There is reason to hope, though. The new ecological consciousness is giving these young provincials second thoughts. They are beginning to treasure the clear air and blue skies of their home towns. The risk of succumbing to galloping inertia in the provinces is far outweighed by the threat of suffocation in the capital. Even the authorities are taking notice. After decades of allowing speculators to destroy landmarks in the city, they have now created an office to restore the buildings and protect them from further vandalism. Thanks to this official change of heart, enough has been preserved to show why in 1803 the German traveler and polymath Alexander von Humboldt was moved to call our capital the City of Palaces.

Details of Altar del Perdon. Precious for its incorruptibility, gold was deemed the only material suitable for the setting for the image of God and his retinue of saints. The fact that gold was being mined nearby helped, producing such jewel boxes as the Camerino della Virgen behind the main altar in the Sanctuary of Ocotlán (Tlaxcala) or the Chapel of the Rosary in the great Dominican convent in Oaxaca. The rich effect of gold ornamentation in high and low relief was achieved by first molding and sculpting in gesso and then covering it with gold leaf. Many of those altarpieces were destroyed during the stormy 19th century by ignorant soldiers, who attacked the columns and niches, thinking they were made of solid gold.

CHAPULTEPEC

One spot of abiding charm is the promontory and castle of Chapultepec, which as every Mexican schoolboy knows, means Grasshopper Hill. Four centuries ago, the hill stood on the western shore of Lake Texcoco. Until fairly recent times, it marked the western limit of the city, but now it is merely the western limit of the downtown area. The castled hilltop rises above a park of *ahuehuetes*, those aged cypresses that are the moss-bearded ancients of the Mexican forest. The park is Mexico's homage to the Bois de Boulogne. The Emperor Maximilian, who gave the castle its present appearance and devoted much attention to the grounds, had much admired the Bois on his first visit to Paris, and sought to reproduce the effect here.

When the Mexicas first arrived in the valley, about seven hundred years ago, they were shunted from one place to the other by the various tribes that were already entrenched on the shore of the lake. The arrogant Toltecs of Culhuacan packed them off to a snake-infested corner of the valley, hoping that would be the end of them. But the Mexicas flourished. They loved snake, and promptly ate up the entire reptile population. The Toltecs heeded the warning and ran the newcomers out.

They ended up in Chapultepec, harassed on all sides by their neighbors. While there, they saw the promised sign of the eagle devouring the serpent – obviously a bird after their own heart – on a little rocky island in the middle of the lake, and there

46

they settled, thus ending their long migration from Atzlan. (From this point onwards, for the convenience of the reader, we shall call the Mexicas by their more familiar name of "Aztecs.")

After the Aztecs had married and bullied their way to power, they looked back on Chapultepec as their homeland. The later emperors liked to return to bathe in its abundant springs. Moctezuma I built an aqueduct to provide his island capital of Tenochtitlán with uncontaminated water. He had his own and his brother's name and portrait carved on the rock face of a hidden grotto. His descendants continued the custom. Moctezuma II, (the one Cortés defeated) also called Xocoyotzin ("the younger" in Náhuatl), went further and brought trees from every corner of his empire to plant in the park, as well as fish and waterfowl to stock the lakes. This is romantically regarded as the precursor of the present Chapultepec Zoo and Botanical Garden.

The conquering Spaniards were not blind to its beauty and utility. They built a chapel on the hilltop and a country retreat for the viceroys in the park below. In 1620 a new aqueduct was built, some of whose arches are still standing on Avenida Chapultepec.

In the eighteenth century, two Gálves viceroys, father and son, built a country house on the top of the hill. After many changes and additions this became the National Military Academy, where the last battle of the Mexican–American war was fought on 13 September, 1847. As we know from a famous engraving of the scene, the Stars and Stripes flew above the National Palace on the following days and was still flying on 15 September, the Mexican Day of Independence.

That war, alas, is not over. It is still being fought in the hearts of Mexicans. Since earliest childhood we are told about the six young-

Sor Juana Inés de la Cruz, New Spain's most famous poet, intellectual and original thinker about women's rights. Oil painting by Miguel Cabrera, 1750. Chapultepec Castle.

Portrait of Don José Maria Morelos y Pavon. Anonymous painter, early 19th century. Chapultepec Castle.

sters, the last of the cadet corps, who died in defense of the castle. They are known as the Child Heroes of Chapultepec. Every year on the anniversary of the battle in which they lost their lives, there is a brief military ceremony in their honor. During roll call, their names are added to the list of the living. As each of their names is called, a sound like a roar is heard. It is every man, woman and child present calling back, "He died for his country!"

A young congressman from Illinois, Abraham Lincoln denounced the Mexican war in the harshest terms, and there were other American voices just as eloquent. Yet the deed was done and to the victor went the spoils, in this case the territory occupied by the present states of California, Arizona, New Mexico, Nevada, Utah and parts of Wyoming and Colorado. That vast territory that Mexico had freed from Spain was therefore now its neighbor's booty.

The war left the country thoroughly demoralized. The Military Academy remained a shambles until another war brought the Austrian Archduke Maximilian to Mexico. He fell instantly in love with Chapultepec and its palace, and that was the end of the Military Academy, for Maximilian swiftly proceeded to turn the old barracks into the sumptuous palace we know. Taking full advantage of its lofty site, Maximilian and his European court architect built turrets and terraces like aeries. To the despair of his treasurer he spent far more than he could afford on his "Mexican Schönbrunn" and increasingly irritated his French and English creditors, especially Napoleon III, who had committed his troops to the support of the Mexican Empire. The Mexican Imperialists, however, found the whole project most satisfactory. They fancied the idea of an imperial court, however improvised. The throne room was hung with chandeliers and gilt mirrors. Another room was lined with malachite. The state apartments contained all the bric-a-brac that any young Hapsburg couple would be expected to have: the silver was Christofle, the furniture, Boulle, the portraits, Winterhalter.

All Maximilian needed now was a shortcut to his office in the National Palace. Remembering Baron Haussmann's lucid remodeling of Paris, he opened a broad, straight causeway across swamps, country lanes and dingy alleys, which ended in a monumental circus at the entrance to the city.

Landscaped along the lines of the Champs Elysées, the avenue was called the *Paseo del Emperador*, the Emperor's Boulevard. With the execution of Maximilian in 1867 the "Emperor's Boulevard" became the *Paseo de la Reforma*, in honor of Juárez's triumphant Reform Laws, separating Church and State. Eventually the castle became the residence of the Mexican president. Porfirio

Díaz, who occupied it longer than any other president, had married an aristocratic Creole and preserved the state apartments more or less as Maximilian and Carlota had left them, except, of course, for the throne room, which he turned into a bowling alley.

President Lázaro Cárdenas (1934–40), a militant populist, refused to be identified with such a place. When he assumed the presidency he moved into *Los Pinos*, a more modest mansion below the ramparts of the castle, where all succeeding presidents have also lived. This was a godsend to the people, for the castle has since been turned into an historical Museum.

Music Room in Chapultepec Castle. The Castle, built in the Second Empire style, now contains an art museum which houses objects that decorated the rooms during the brief reign of Maximilian and Carlota in the later half of the 19th century.

THE ZÓCALO

The traditional center of the city, towards which Maximilian had directed his Parisian boulevard from Chapultepec, covered roughly, during its first four hundred years, the area of the Aztec Tenochtitlán and the Spanish city that Cortés built on its ruins. Its focal point is the Zócalo, an open square formed in Aztec times by the coming together of the four causeways that provided access to the shores of Lake Texcoco. In the present-day Zócalo, the National Palace encloses the entire east side of the square. It has been the seat of executive power ever since Moctezuma II built his palace there circa 1502, which makes it the oldest consecutive seat of government in the hemisphere. Diagonally opposite the National Palace, the cathedral majestically closes off the northern end of the square. It stands adjacent to the spot where the Aztec's Great Teocalli ("House of the Gods") once stood.

The Tenochtitlán that Cortés and his men found in 1519 was a city very much like Venice in its early days. It was built out of a few islands formed by dredging the bottom of the lagoon. The tactical advantage was obvious: Lake Texcoco provided them with the biggest moat in the world. Canals both divided and united the different *barrios* (quarters) and canoes provided the transportation. According to contemporary accounts, Tenochtitlán was an extraordinarily beautiful city, with gardens bordering the canals, thriving commerce, crowded marketplaces and magnificent palaces. Moctezuma had a botanical garden in his own palace as well as a zoo with freaks, dwarfs, hunchbacks and animals housed in an enormous establishment on the western edge of the city. The population was an estimated five hundred thousand, and to the Spaniards approaching along the Ixtapalapa causeway from the south it must

Oil painting of the Zócalo, late 18th century.

have seemed that the entire population had turned out to see their arrival. The rooftops were black with people and canoes crowded the waters on either side of the road. The horses filled the onlookers with awe. They thought the horsemen were precisely that: horse–men. (In Tlaxcala, during a banquet, the natives had offered the horses hot chocolate and turkey *tacos*.)

Moctezuma came out to meet the Spaniards with his retinue. His magnificence was vividly described by Bernal Díaz del Castillo, the soldier–chronicler who set down his experiences many years later. Nothing escaped Díaz: the gem-encrusted gold soles of Moctezuma's sandals, the reverently downcast eyes of the noble lords who waited on him, the canopy of green feathers worked in gold and silver and fringed with pearls and turquoise. Cortés stepped forward to embrace the Emperor but was restrained by Moctezuma's attendant lords. So he simply presented the Emperor with a necklace of colored beads strung on a musk-scented golden cord. Though Bernal does not report Moctezuma's words of greeting, they have been preserved for us in the Florentine Codex. Clearly, Moctezuma was convinced he was welcoming the Lord Quetzalcóatl in the person of Cortés. He led the Spaniard and his followers to his father Axayatl's palace on the western side of the square and retired to his own on the opposite side, where the National Palace now stands.

This peaceful interlude did not last long. Eighteen months and many battles later, the Spaniards and their Indian allies – with a fleet of brigantines built in Tlaxcala and portered up piecemeal to Texcoco – laid siege to Tenochtitlán. The beleaguered Aztecs destroyed causeways, bridges, houses, everything that could be of any value to the besiegers. They buried their idols and dumped their sacred stones into wells. When Tenochtitlán fell, the Spaniards found a city of rubble and rotting corpses. The stench forced them to return to Coyoacán; the Tlaxcalans remained to feast that night on the limbs of their defeated enemies .

Cortés ordered the reconstruction of the Aztec capital along the lines of a Spanish city. His architect designed a grid more or less following the canals and centered on the intersection of the four causeways. The central city was reserved for Spaniards, and the Indians were sent literally beyond the pale. The canals were filled in and eventually the lake itself was drained to avoid the periodic and disastrous floods. Inevitably, the land filled in between the original islands was soggy. Just how soggy can be deduced from the swaybacked cornices and roof-lines of many a colonial building: the prime example is relatively new, the Palace of Fine Arts, which has sunk several feet below street level. (Modern engineering has solved the problem by using pilings or "floating" foundations.)

Detail of the façade of the chapel of La Conchita Coyoacan, in early colonial style with marked Moorish influence.

Iturbide Palace. Lithograph by Casimiro Castro, early 19th century.

A corner of the Iturbide Palace patio.

Opposite page: Iturbide Palace. Detail with stone frame, a typical mix of Baroque doorway, Moorish door and Churigueresque pilasters.

THE NATIONAL PALACE

National Palace. Still used by the present-day federal government, the palace was built on the foundation of Moctezuma's palace and was both the Viceroy's residence and seat of the New Spain government. Every year the Grito de Dolores – the cry of Independence – is reenacted by the President from the central balcony.

For political reasons, Cortés insisted on building the capital of New Spain directly on top of the Aztec capital. It would not do to move elsewhere and leave the natives free to return to the site of their ancient allegiances. The land itself was endowed with spiritual authority, so the true source and seat of power must remain where it had always been. For the same reason, Cortés built his own palace on the site and foundation of Moctezuma's.

In 1692 Indian rioters set fire to the palace (there was no corn, no money, and a suspicion of hidden stores in the palace itself). The damage to the building was soon repaired, but the sur-

roundings remained squalid beyond belief. Contemporary records tell us about public latrines and vegetable stalls next to each other in the middle of the square. In 1789, almost a century after the Indian riot, a recently arrived viceroy, the second Count Revillagigedo, a man of the Enlightenment, was shocked by the filth he saw and smelled from his windows, and set about cleaning up the mess. He cleared away the stalls and the itinerant merchants, ordered the level of the square to be lowered, then paved it and fitted it with covered gutters for sewage and rainwater. During these excavations, the old Aztec calendar stone came to light, undoubtedly part of the sacred treasure the Aztecs had concealed during the last days of Tenochtitlán.

In 1793, during the same viceroy's term of office, the square as we know it was taking shape, with the south and west sides much as they are now. Mexico City was at the peak of prosperity at the time. It was the golden age of the *hacienda* and the wealth of the second silver boom was not yet dissipated. The *hacendados* and the mining millionaires, as well as the merchants and bankers who married into the aristocracy, showed their wealth by building palaces and endowing convents, hospitals, schools and churches in the capital.

Like all wars, the struggle for Independence brought disorder, poverty, and destruction from 1810 to 1821. No renaissance followed the peace; instead there was a series of revolutions and palace coups from which Mexico has never entirely recovered.

When independence was finally achieved, the spotlight of history turned away from the National Palace to blaze upon the nearby Palace of the Marquess de Jaral de Berrio. It was then occupied by a conservative Creole officer, Agustín de Iturbide. Alarmed at the liberal turn that post–Napoleonic politics were taking in Spain, he decided to join forces with the insurgent leaders to effect the definitive break with Spain in 1821. The Decree of Independence was ceremoniously signed in the palace he occupied.

Iturbide showed his colors soon enough. He made himself Emperor, granting himself and his family huge possessions and impressive cash rewards. He insisted upon being addressed as "His Most Serene Highness" and adopted all the Napoleonic trappings of empire. Thus arrayed, he and his wife posed for countless portraits. A scant year later, he was tumbled from his pasteboard throne and sent into exile by the rebellious Antonio Lopéz de Santa Anna.

A theater named after President Santa Anna. Oil painting by Pedro Gualdi, 19th century.

55

Patio of the Convento de las Vizcainas. Built in the 18th century, the Convento was a refuge for widows and orphan girls of Basque origin. Oil painting by Augustín Ilizaliturri, 19th century.

Church dome and cupola of the Convento de las Vizcainas.

When Iturbide's brief empire came to a close, the National Palace once again became the residence of the head of state. But the palace is too old and has served too many masters to have come through history unscathed. It is too big, and has always been too densely populated, teeming at all hours with equerries and maids and pages and soldiers and ladies–in–waiting and ushers and body–guards, and today with motorcyclists and secretaries and helicopter pilots and applicants for jobs and official favors. One can imagine almost anything happening in the more florid periods of its past. Even Maximilian, a rather insipid paragon of a prince, turns out to have had a little side door for certain court ladies. His infidelities were no secret. In the country that invented machismo, even the Emperor had to prove that he could be unfaithful. Now, however, under an uninterrupted series of PRI presidents, the palace has become increasingly strait–laced and formal, even as the city around it bursts at the seams with teeming life.

Opposite page: Magnificently restored Churrigueresque altar in the Convento de las Vizcainas.

*Baroque Church of San Juan de Dios, designed in 1729 by
Miguel Custio Durán. The façade with its shell canopy is
attached to the bell tower. The church shares a delightful
plaza with the Franz Mayer Museum next door.*

Patio of the Franz Mayer Museum, previously the Hospital of San Juan de Dios, the most important infirmary in Mexico City during the 18th century.

At left, the façade of the Royal Mining Seminary, a splendid neo-classical building by Manuel Tolsà, 1797-1811. Adjoining it, in the foreground, is the main post office, by Adamo Boari begun in 1902.

Main staircase of the Royal Mining Seminary, an example of neo-classical architecture.

61

The Baroque Pocito Chapel, 18th century, by Francisco Guerrero y Torres, is tucked in behind the old Basilica of Guadalupe. The tile covered cupola shows the influence of the "Poblano" style.

Interior of La Enseñanza Church, a Baroque masterpiece of the 18th century.

Every city with a history is palimpsest to the trained eye. The scarred remains of ancient cultures, old wars and modern revolutions, or failed monarchies and acts of God, are either refurbished, demolished or paved over and put to modern use. A buried baby pyramid lay unsuspected for several centuries until discovered during the construction of the subway. It is now part of a Metro station.

Detail of tragineras, boats typical of the Xachimilco canals.

The palace from whose balcony the aristocratic insurgent and liberator Augustín de Iturbide proclaimed the establishment of the First Empire (with himself as emperor) lost the name of its original owners and is now known as the Palacio de Iturbide. It is now a branch of the powerful Banco Nacional de Mexico.

Fortunately, the late 20th century has not been allowed to show its face here, in the historic heart of Mexico City. Nonetheless, its affluence appears in the cleaned-up facades and the discreet adaptation of certain unfortunate buildings to the simplicity of its more ordinary historical neighbors.

The irrepressible brashness of new money and modernist ideas makes itself felt in the post-modernist building boom that starts where the thoroughfare coming from the Zocalol joins forces with the wide, tree-lined Reforma. This once serene boulevard was developed during the 30-year period of stability that ended with the 1910 Revolution. It exuded nostalgia for the Parisian boulevards of that period and lasted just long enough for the many rich refugees from World War II to feel they were not too far from home.

Opposite page: A powerful ring of concrete blocks surrounding the crater of an extinct volcano in the heart of Mexico City. Collective work by Helen Escobedo, Sebastián, Federico Silva, Manuel Felguérez, Mathias Goeritz, 1978-80.

But it was the very influx of money and talent brought by those refugees that ended up razing the charming *hôtels particuliers* in order to build the huge glass skyscrapers that have turned Mexico D.F. into a city of mirrors – towering mirrors with heliports on their roofs. The few old hôtels left standing are now occupied by banks, clubs or brokerage houses.

Following Reforma west, past the Castle of Chapultepec, the museums and the posh hotels, another enclave of entrenched wealth appears in the residential area built in the hills and ravines of Bosque de las Lomas. The architecture is too eclectic and idiosyncratic to achieve any sort of style. There is even a domineering glass-floored house teetering over the edge of a cliff. The most impressive thing about this development is the money behind it.

Though Luis Barragán, the poet of Mexican architecture, left a school of fervent disciples, among them the great Ricardo Legoretta (Hotel Camino Real, Mexico City), his kind of architecture is now more visible in the provinces, especially in the luxury seaside resorts like Cancún. Another modern master, Pedro Ramirez Vázquez, creator of the Museum of Anthropology, the new Basilica of the Virgin of Guadalupe, and the Plaza de las Tres Culturas, continues to build on a monumental scale both in Mexico and in Europe.

But the newest and most impressive extension of the sky developed beyond the end of Reforma, on the road to Toluca, is an area known as Santa Fe, where the pervasive mall culture of the U.S. pitched its most impressive tent. It started with some of the big downtown department stores and, practically overnight, a congress of residential and office skyscrapers mushroomed on either side of the road.

The pervading style can best be characterized as "drop dead" modern, though it is far from silent. But then you are not in the city for tranquillity, but for the bustle and what used to be called the urban symphony, the rush of the gung-ho spirit that creates cultures and great cities. And that is what you can find in modern Mexico.

The Main Library at the University City, with Juan O'Gorman's mosaic mural, reputed to be the largest in the world.

Modern stone sculpture in the garden of La Noria: the Dolores Olmedo Foundation.

Olga and Rufino Tamayo Garden. The bronze sculpture is by Rufino Tamayo.

66

Above left: The Mexican Stock Exchange, towering over the Reforma Avenue, was designed by architect Juan José Diaz Infante, in collaboration with Heriberto Izquierdo, Raul Izquierdo, Ricardo Zamora and Enrique Ross.

Above right: Arcos Torre I, finished in 1997 by architects Teodoro González de Leon and Francisco Serrano.

265 Reforma Avenue, finished in 1996 by Sergio Breceda Ceceña of the architectural firm of Levy, Harari, Breceda y Asociados.

*Opposite page: Façade of
the Frida Kahlo Museum.*

*Patio built by Mexican
architect Luis Barragan.*

Opposite page: National Museum of Anthropology.
Detail of sculpture at the Centro Cultural Universitario.

National Museum of Anthropology, designed by Pedro
Ramirez Vázquez. The immense "umbrella" fountain in the
courtyard is dedicated to the Aztec god, Tlaloc.

CHAPTER 2

The Route of Cortés

*Yucatan. Chichén Itzá. Temple of the Warriors
and Group of the Thousand Columns,
Maya-Toltec culture (after 950 A.D.).*

The Discovery of Mexico

The first recorded sighting of what is now Mexico occurred in 1517. Bernal Díaz del Castillo was the chronicler of the first expeditions and the *Conquest of New Spain*, as he called his book, is still the best guide to the subject. Three boats under the command of the rich Miguel Hidalgo who financed the expedition reached the north-eastern coast of Yucatán twenty-one days after leaving Cuba. Sighting a large settlement with white stone temples, they were convinced that they had reached Cathay, the land of the Great Khan, so they named the city "the Great Cairo."

The first two expeditions failed to gain a foothold on the mainland. The second expedition, under Juan de Grijalva, brought back enough gold trinkets taken from the Indians of Tabasco to make Diego Velázquez, the governor of Cuba and financial backer of the expedition, a rich man. The glint of gold worked up enormous enthusiasm for further explorations. Velázquez set about organizing a third expedition. He put up part of the money, but as he had no intention of leading it personally, he looked about for a partner who would put up the rest and take charge of the entire venture. Many aspirants came forward. In the end, Velázquez settled on Cortés, against the advice of his courtiers.

Since dropping out of Salamanca, Cortés had led the picaresque existence typical of a poor *hidalgo's* son, whose ambitions far exceeded his means. He shipped out to Cuba, eventually settling down in the eastern city of Santiago. In time he made a modest fortune farming, mining and acting as a free-lance lawyer on the side.

This was hardly the life he had dreamed of. In 1519 he was thirty-four years old; his time was running short. So when Velázquez chose him to head the third expedition, he mortgaged his lands and houses, sold his Indians, and invested the total proceeds in the eleven-boat expedition. Velázquez began to have misgivings. As the date of departure approached, Cortés was warned that

Velázquez was replacing him, so he set forth before the appointed day and thereby foiled the governor's plans.

The official purpose of the expedition was to record events and map the western seas; to rescue Christians from a 1517 sortie who were reputedly held in captivity; to win the Indians over to the service of His Most Catholic Majesty, Charles V; to instruct them in the Christian faith, "and as a sign of submission to him to send great quantities of gold, gems, pearls and other things that they might have...."

Reaching the island of Cozumel, east of Yucatán, Cortés set about tracking down the shipwrecked Spaniards. Only two had survived. Of the two survivors, one had taken a native wife and had sired several children who thus became the first true Mestizos in the land. He had gone completely native and had no desire to leave his family. The second, the cleric Jerónimo de Aguilar, had remained celibate. When he presented himself before Cortés in a canoe full of Indians, Cortés asked, "Where is the Spaniard?" One of the naked, sunburnt men, with only a loincloth "to cover his shame" spoke up: *"Soy yo,"* he said. Even his accent was strange. He unwrapped a small Book of Hours from a bundle of tattered clothes as proof of his identity. Cortés took him aboard, gave him "Christian" clothing, and from that moment on, Aguilar, with his knowledge of the Mayan language and customs, became an invaluable assistant.

The expedition then sailed along the coast of Yucatán toward the mainland until reaching the great Grijalva River of Tabasco, named after the Spanish captain who had discovered it. It was on that occasion that the natives had shown themselves to be so friendly, and had given Grijalva and his men the gold which had so excited Velázquez and the other Spaniards in Cuba. Now, however, they were definitely hostile, and Cortés, landing, had to fight his first battle, in

Arrival of Cortés in Veracruz by Diego Rivera.

which he acquitted himself like a seasoned campaigner. The Indians were defeated by their own ceremonial approach to war as much as by the surprise of Spanish firearms and horses. They jumped and yelled instead of attacking, throwing fistfuls of dust and leaves up into the air to conceal their dead comrades from the enemy.

The Indians finally surrendered. Gifts changed hands – glass beads for gold again, and twenty slave women "to cook" for the Spaniards on their boat. When asked where the gold came from, the Indians pointed west, repeating the words "Culhua" and "Mexico," which meant nothing even to Aguilar. The Spaniards left on Palm Sunday after mass. The slave women were baptized. Then, to the Indians' astonishment, one by one the iron warriors kissed a cross made of fresh-cut saplings before they returned to the boat. Thus Cortés, his mercenarian chaplain and his soldiers established the ritual they were to follow after every landing and every victory in the course of the Conquest of Mexico.

THE FOUNDING OF VERACRUZ

The best gift Cortés was ever to receive was an inquisitive, restless, good–looking slave woman, who pestered Aguilar, asking for the names and uses of things. Her own name was Malinali, so they baptized her Marina, which was as close as they could get to it in Spanish. Her usefulness was not recognized until they reached the deso–late sand dunes of what is now Veracruz. There Cortés, landing again, finally came face to face with Moctezuma's ambassadors. Nobody under–stood a word they said except for Marina. They spoke Náhuatl, her native tongue. She translated into Maya, and Aguilar then passed it on in Spanish. But her resourcefulness far exceeded her usefulness as a translator. After Veracruz, she became indispensable to Cortés, whose bed she came to share, as well as his thoughts. She was wily, tactful, possessive. By her desire to please the Spaniard, she turned herself into a diplomat of genius. She presented him to the natives in the best possible light, lacing his proposals with the euphemisms and compliments that still constitute the most effective passport for Mexican travel. After his eventual triumph, Cortés gave Doña Marina a handsome settlement and married her off to one of his own men, Juan de Jaramillo, who is recorded as having got almost too drunk to attend his own wedding. Mexico remembers

Marina with great cruelty as a betrayer of her people, conveniently forgetting that her own people had sold her into slavery.

In Veracruz, Moctezuma's ambassadors failed to persuade Cortés to take the Emperor's gifts and go away. In a last desperate attempt, Moctezuma sent Cortés those treasures which were soon to astonish Europe. It was, of course, exactly the wrong thing to do. Nothing could persuade the Spaniards to turn back after they had seen the gold and silver jewelry spread out on the sand, and a helmet full of gold.

Realizing their mistake, the Aztec ambassadors disappeared as unexpectedly as they had come. The Spaniards faced a dilemma. To remain in the vast emptiness could mean death either by starvation or on the sacrificial altars of the obviously powerful Moctezuma. To return to Cuba meant sacrificing honor, glory and treasure to Velázquez, and probably being excluded from future expeditions. The stranded Spaniards were divided between those who were loyal to Velázquez and those who urged Cortés to conquer the land, though this was not the expedition's purpose.

Taking a legalistic line, Cortés found a way to bow to the will of the latter group, which coincided nicely with his own ambitions. He called on the expedition's scrivener to testify that on a certain day – and he chose Good Friday as being suitable – the Rich City of the True Cross (Veracruz) was founded in the name of Their Most Catholic Majesties. Older men were chosen, and as the new city lay outside Velázquez's jurisdiction, Cortés, whose authority derived from Velázquez, formally tendered his resignation. The City Council accepted it, considered the situation, and presently summoned Cortés to inform him that they he had been elected Chief Justice and Captain General, agreeing also to give him a fifth of the expedition's proceeds after the deduction of the royal fifth. The whole thing went like clockwork.

A few days after the Aztecs had vanished, other Indians appeared who inadvertently showed Cortés the way to defeat Moctezuma. These Totonac Indians, sent by the Fat Cacique of nearby Cempoala, informed Cortés that the Aztecs were hated throughout the land. The Fat Cacique – so fat he could not come personally to greet the Spaniards – begged them to visit him in Cempoala. Cortés accepted and lived to bless the day. The Fat Cacique became his first and greatest ally.

After that, the events came thick and fast. Five arrogant ambassadors from Moctezuma arrived to scold the Fat Cacique for befriending Cortés, and demanded twenty sacrificial victims to erase the affront. Cortés prevailed on his host to take the Aztecs as prisoners and give them a sound thrashing. "The act was so astonishing," Bernal tells us, "that they said it must be the work of *teules*, which means gods or demons," a name which stuck to the Spaniards. The same night, Cortés himself freed two of the prisoners and sent them off to Moctezuma as living proof of his good faith.

The Cempoalans were terrified by the possible consequences of their actions. Cortés promised to defend them if they would swear fealty to Charles V, which they immediately did. The Fat Cacique then offered Cortés a fat princess, his own niece, as a bride, and seven other maidens for his men. Cortés accepted on one condition, that the Cempoalans abjure their idols, forbid the prostitution of boys dressed as women, and accept Christ as their Lord. The Fat Cacique and the priests agreed to see what could be done about sodomy, but on no account would they give up their gods. At this, Cortés and his men swarmed up the pyramids and demolished their idols while the Cempoalans cowered below in terror. When nothing happened – the sun went on shining, the earth did not swallow them up – the Cempoalans recovered their spirits and embraced the Spaniards affectionately.

News from Cuba reached Cortés in Cempoala. Velázquez was in a fury. He was trying to bring influence to bear on the Spanish court, Velázquez's friends plotted to desert Cortés and steal away on one of the ships. It was then, faced with the possibility of defection, that Cortés "burned his boats," in the traditional phrase, though in fact he only ran them aground and dismantled their rigging.

The Spaniards left Cempoala in August, 1519. They could move more easily now; the Fat Cacique had provided them with many bearers. They climbed up toward the central plateau by way of Jalapa. The intense cold was something they had not foreseen. In Xocatlán, a city loyal to the Aztecs, they found "more than one hundred thousand skulls" neatly piled in the temple square. The local Cacique tried to make Cortés turn back by describing the greatness and power of Moctezuma. But his descriptions of Moctezuma's treasure only made the Spaniards forget their cold and hunger in their eagerness to reach Tenochtitlán.

THE TLAXCALAN CAMPAIGN

The independent seigniory of Tlaxcala, correctly described by the Cempoalans as the principal enemy of the Aztec Empire, proved to be every bit as hostile to the Spaniards. Having successfully resisted all Aztec attempts to conquer them, they had no intention of surrendering their independence to others. "There were so many warriors that they could have blinded us just with fistfuls of earth," said Bernal. They fought rather more cleverly than that, giving battle in such broken terrain that the Spaniards' horses were of little use. They killed a mare to show that the horses were not immortal. In short, they set about disproving the supposed divinity of the Spanish. Several inconclusive battles took place before the Tlaxcalans sued for peace.

News of the Spanish victory over the hitherto undefeated Tlaxcalans flashed across the land. Five Aztec nobles immediately appeared in Cortés's camp. Aside from the usual gifts, they brought dire warnings of the Tlaxcalans' treachery, and the surprising news that Moctezuma was willing to submit to Charles V and send him a yearly tribute providing that the Spaniards stayed away from Tenochtitlán.

The Tlaxcalan elders, for their part, begged him to visit their city. They provided five hundred bearers for his cannon and calmed his suspicions by offering themselves and their families as hostages. Cortés finally accepted and Tlaxcala received the Spaniards with a joyful celebration. The Tlaxcalans offered their noblest maidens to the Spaniards. As he had done before in Cempoala, Cortés refused unless they agreed to abjure their idols and adopt Christianity. Being more spirited than the Cempoalans, the Tlaxcalans refused so brusquely that the mercenarian chaplain advised Cortés to let them be.

The most Cortés was able to achieve for the time being was the use of a newly whitewashed temple for the Virgin Mary and the christening of the Tlaxcalan princesses, who were given such peninsular names as Doña Luisa and Doña Elvira and then parceled out to his captains. Cortés destroyed the cages where men and women were being fattened for sacrifice, as he did afterwards in every town he entered.

A tug-of-war now ensued between Moctezuma's ambassadors and the Tlaxcalan elders. Each sought to win Cortés's trust. Moctezuma, fearing an alliance between the Spaniards and Tlaxcalans, sought to effect a separation as soon as possible. He proffered a courtly invitation to Tenochtitlán and suggested that Cortés take the road through Cholula, where he and his men would be well looked after. The Tlaxcalans told him it was a trap. He should take the road through Huejotzingo, a town held by loyal friends and allies.

After much deliberation, Cortés chose the road through Cholula. The Tlaxcalans, though hurt by this sign of mistrust, offered an escort of ten thousand men, assuring him that he would need them. Cortés accepted only one thousand.

Cholula was a beautiful city of towers and temples. It was the sacred city of Anahuac, and the Tlaxcalans refused to enter it. Cortés and his captains were lodged in a palace with a large courtyard, but shortly after their arrival they saw that they had indeed been tricked by Moctezuma. They were provided with firewood and water, but no food. Nor did the local chieftain appear to welcome them. More ambassadors arrived from Moctezuma, now insolently ordering Cortés to go no further.

The Tlaxcalans sent word that twenty thousand warriors were deployed in the countryside to slaughter the Spaniards. Doña Marina, talking to an old Cholulan woman, confirmed the rumor. The Cholulans had even sacrificed seven Indians to ensure the success of their plans.

Cortés lost no time. He announced to the Cholulans that he was leaving early the next morning and would need two thousand porters to accompany him to Tenochtitlán. The Cholulan nobles, priests and warriors were laughing, Bernal says, when they gathered in the forecourt of Cortés's palace the following morning. Their glee vanished when Cortés, interpreted by Aguilar and Marina, spoke to them from astride his horse. He itemized the details of their plot against him, mentioning even the pots of salt, chili peppers and tomatoes waiting to spice the flesh of the twenty live Spaniards who were to be sacrificed in a ceremony of Thanksgiving. He upbraided them for their treacherous methods. The priests and caciques admitted the truth of these accusations, adding that they were merely obeying their lord Moctezuma. After hearing their confession, Cortés gave the signal. A shot was fired, and the slaughter began. Musket and cannon were emptied into the ranks of the Cholulans. The killing spread through the city, and temples and towers were set on fire. The carnage, fuelled by the Tlaxcalans' ancient enmity to the Cholulans, was so atrocious that Cortés had to intercede in their favor. When a semblance of order was restored, Cortés pronounced his usual homily to the Indians, ordered the town to be whitewashed, and set up a cross as proof of the impotence of the Mexican idols before the power of the Christian God. After Cholula, there could be no further doubt about Moctezuma's intentions.

The fact that the Spaniards were obviously mortals and not gods had not entirely dispelled the idea that Cortés might still be Quetzalcóatl's avatar. After all, the Plumed Serpent in his time had also appeared in human guise. Now, as Cortés approached the valley of Anahuac, a comet appeared and flared nightly above Tenochtitlán; while the volcano Popocatépetl spouted a vertical column of black smoke.

When the Spaniards crossed the pass between the volcanoes and descended toward the city on the lagoon, Moctezuma yielded to his fate. He donned his fine cotton cloak, his gem-studded sandals, his tiara of gold and, accompanied by the noblest lords of the realm, he walked to receive Cortés, begging him to enter and rest himself and take possession of his city.

THE NEIGHBORING REPUBLIC OF YUCATÁN: THE STATES OF YUCATÁN, CAMPECHE AND QUINTANA ROO

Mexicans affectionately refer to the whole of the Yucatán peninsula as "The Neighboring Republic of Yucatán," (though it now comprises the three separate states of Yucatán, Campeche and Quintana Roo) which suggests Mayan ruins and the charming "white city" of Mérida.

Campeche (from the Maya, *kam*, snake, and *pech*, tick – not an inviting place name) provided the door through which the Spaniards finally entered and conquered Yucatán. The east and north coasts of the peninsula proved impregnable. Montejo the Younger, a son of one of Cortés's captains, was left with the task of colonizing the area after his father had given up in despair; he first fortified himself in Tabasco and, when he had achieved the necessary strength, launched his ultimately successful assault on the Mayan bastions of the peninsula.

From the beginning, a bitter rivalry existed between the fortified port of Campeche and the inland city of Mérida. The Campechanos resented the political domination of the northern city. As the doorway to the peninsula, Campeche had to withstand the constant attacks of pirates during colonial times and, after Independence, even an attack from Santa Anna's navy in 1842. After much political maneuvering and a genocidal struggle between the Mayas and the rest of the population, Campeche finally achieved statehood in 1858.

Quintana Roo. Tulum. Above: El Castillo and facing page: an overview of the ruins. The only pre-Hispanic monument built by the sea. Abandoned in 1544 and practically lost in the jungle.

Quintana Roo, on the eastern flank of the peninsula, did not become a state until 1974, though the federal government had separated it in 1902 from Yucatán, whose government had proved unable to cope with the sporadic and fierce rebellions in the area, where most of the unsubdued Mayas of the War of the Castes had taken refuge.

The modern state of Yucatán has thus been reduced to a triangular territory of calcareous rock, sinkholes and Mayan ruins in the north of the peninsula. It has consolations, though. Quintana Roo can boast of Cancún, Túlum and Cozumel; Campeche, of its precious woods and offshore oil, but Yucatán has kept its character and its people, the ineffable *yucatecos*, a people of great, if loony, charm.

Physically and culturally they form a race apart. Though descended from the Maya, they did not inherit the elegantly tapered profiles preserved in classic Mayan art. The likeliest explanation of the difference is that classic art portrayed princes, priests and warriors of high breeding, whose heads were artificially shaped from birth to an ideal standard of beauty. Babies' heads were banded soon after birth to produce the characteristic elongation of the profile, while a bead of turquoise or jade was placed on one side of the bridge on the nose to tease the baby's eye inwards. However strange this description may sound, the results were stunningly beautiful, as may be seen in the carved heads of Palenque and Copán, or the clay statuettes of Jaina. This beauty did not, however, denote any great degree of amiability, which is the essential trait of the present day *yucateco*. When other regional stereo-

types are discussed, the more notable defects are pointed out along with their virtues. Thus the diligent and devout *poblano* (from Puebla) is thought hypocritical; the cheery and entertaining *jarocho* (from Veracruz) can be coarse; the *regiomontano* (from Monterrey) an admirable citizen and empire–builder, is stingier than a Scot; the *tapatio*, from Jalisco, is one hell of a guy, but carries the macho chip on his shoulder at all times; the *norteño*, from the northern border states is as open–handed as he is open–minded, but an inverted snob, proud to be a bronco. Only the yucateco has escaped invidious classification. His countryman readily agree that he is bright, slightly nutty, and totally sympathetic.

The traveler can drive from the posh seaside resort of Cancún to that most poetic of Mayan ruins, the seaside temple of Tulúm perched on a cliff above the Caribbean. He can bathe in the magical lagoons or watch the chewing gum trees grow, for the southern jungle of Yucatán is the source of most of the *chicle* chewed in world today. The chico zapote (*Achras zapota*), or sapodilla tree, grows forty to fifty feet high, has glossy small leaves and the most delicious fruit imaginable. The chewing–gum is made from the rubbery latex drawn from its trunk. Chewing chicle has been a Maya habit since prehistoric times. General Santa Anna introduced chewing–gum to the United States when he was held prisoner in Washington after his defeat at San Jacinto. The young Captain Adams, detailed to keep watch on him, observed that he was constantly chewing something that he never swallowed. Santa Anna offered him a piece from a small loaf he carried in his pocket and an American habit was born.

But the phrase "The Neighboring Republic of Yucatán" is not a joke. It is a historical fact. Yucatán – the whole peninsula – did secede from Mexico in 1839 to form an independent state, something it could not afford. In 1847, The War of the Castes, aimed at the extermination of all the Creoles and Mestizos, exploded among the Maya in Yucatán. Since Mexico was then at war with the U.S., the secessionists could

Yucatan. Chichén Itzá was the most brilliant political and cultural center in the Yucatan plain. Temple of the Warriors, in front of the temple of Chacmool, positioned between two feathered serpent columns.

Yucatan. Chichén Itzá. The Ball Court is one of the largest in the Maya area.

Yucatan. Chichén Itzá. The Castle or Pyramid of Kukulcan, a magnificent Toltex influenced structure, with four staircases and a small temple on top.

expect no help from that quarter. Desperate appeals were sent from Mérida and Campeche to Washington, London, even Spain, vainly offering Yucatán to which ever government could provide immediate military aid. The rebels were at the same time getting arms and rum from the English in Belize, so it was not very realistic to solicit help from London. Only the coming of the rains put an end to this first and most violent onslaught of the War of the Castes. The rebels went back to plant their fields before taking up arms again. By that time, peace had been reestablished between the United States and Mexico (1848), and the central

government was able to send Yucatán help against the rebels. As a result of this, Yucatán finally and definitively rejoined the republic.

Yucatán's offer of its sovereignty to foreign powers is not as disloyal as it seems. After all, it had little reason to consider itself part of Mexico. Yucatán was not conquered by Cortés but by agents of the Spanish Crown. Its close political links with Mexico dated only from 1821. Given its history, Yucatán developed a strongly independent, there-fore federalist, spirit. When Mexico became mono-lithically centralist between 1835 and 1846, Yucatán rebelled and, following the example of Texas, broke relations with the central government in 1839.

Yucatan. Chichén Itzá. Temple of the Warriors, head of staircase.

Yucatan. Chichén Itzá. The Nunnery, a name given by the Spanish in the 16th century, as it contained small rooms believed to be inhabited by priestesses.

Yucatan. Uxmal.
General view with
the Governor's
Palace in the far left.

The War of the Castes lasted long after 1848, though it never again came so near to winning its objective. About two-thirds of the population of Yucatán perished in the initial years of the war. The surviving rebels retreated to the south-eastern jungles, where they continued to receive rum and bad advice from the British. They refused to sign a truce with the government of Yucatán, declaring they would govern themselves according to their ancient customs. They did, however, promise not to attack Creoles. They had given Queen Victoria their word and intended to keep it.

The Agricultural Revolution that took place in the United States was to benefit Yucatan. In 1875, George Appleby invented the twine binder for use with the machine-harvested cereals. The demand for binder twine was enormous. Its supply was found in the henequen agave, which grew wild in the Yucatán. Since the twine was shipped out of the port of Sisal, this became the generic name for any agave fiber. The sisal fortunes created an atmosphere of prosperity in the cities and of European luxury in the town houses of the hacendados. The Revolution in 1910, the subsequent Agrarian Reforms, and in the mid-twentieth century, the invention of synthetic fibers all contributed to the death of the twine industry. So the state of Yucatán, which once lorded it over the entire province, is now the poor relation living on subsidies from the federal government. Even chewing gum is now synthetic. On the other hand, the islands and beaches of Quintana Roo have become international tourist attractions. Campeche has oil, shrimp fisheries and cattle. Yucatán, like an impoverished aristocrat, has kept its pedigree and its traditions, the underground lagoons and sacred grottoes, the richest ruins and the poorest lands.

Yucatan. Uxmal. The oval Pyramid of the Magician, also known as the Pyramid of the Dwarf or of the Sorcerer. Construction was begun in the sixth century A.D. and took around 400 years to build, during which five temples were built, one over the other.

*Yucatan. Uxmal. "Juego de la Pelota." Detail of
the court where the sacred ball game took place
in which both winners and losers risked their
lives. The game was brought by the Toltecs to the
Yucatan peninsula.*

Yucatan. Uxmal. Decoration on the wall of the Nunnery. The geometrical fret work of the stone face can be found only in certain southern cultures such as the Maya and the Mixtecs Indians in Oaxaca.

TABASCO

Most of Tabasco is flat, and moreover wet. Bounded and irrigated by the two largest river systems in the country, the Usumacinta and the Grijalva, Tabasco has been called the Mexican Mesopotamia. Until roads were built in the 1950's, the villages and towns of that waterlogged state formed a kind of inland archipelago. The shaded groves of cacao, the chocolate bean, which was used as currency throughout the land, have continued to flourish as they did when Cortés and Bernal Díaz first wrote about them.

After the revolution, Tabasco grew fat like its cattle and its cattlemen. The oil boom of the late 'seventies put an end to its tranquility. Oil poured money into the state, creating thousands of jobs, and outrageous prices for food and shelter. Even the landscape has changed, slashed by the pipelines, airstrips and new roads connecting the oil fields. Herds of plump, pale Brahma cattle, attended by the flocks of snowy egrets that perch on them for ticks, now graze near giant gas flares erupting from fields and lagoons. The sheer activity of the airport in Villahermosa, the state capital, is an indication of the change .

Tabasco, then, has been rich and poor and is now rich again. To those who believe that the Word outlasts Wealth, however, Tabasco will never again be considered poor. It produced two of the greatest Mexican poets of this century, Carlos Pellicer and José Gorostiza. Pellicer was born in 1899, Gorostiza in 1901 – one a tropical imagist, dripping with color, the other an austere metaphysical poet. Together they represent the flesh and the mind of the Mexican spirit.

Tabasco. Villahermosa. Los Cedros, the park designed by Alejandro Yabur.

Tabasco. Villahermosa. La Venta Park.
These colossal Olmec heads, belonging to
the Olmec culture, mother culture of
Mesoamerica. They were the largest
sculptures in the Western hemisphere and
could weigh up to 20 tons. Each was
hewn from a single stone brought by
rafts from as far as 100 miles away and
each had distinguishing features.

*Tabasco. Villahermosa. Memorial Garrido
designed by Teodoro Gonzáles de Leon.*

93

*Tabasco. Jalapa. Las Animas. Kiosk
used as a bandstand, a traditional
feature in municipal gardens.*

Tabasco. Jalapa. The arched verandah at the Hacienda El Lencero, once home of the very controversial president during the American war, Antonio Lopez de Santa Anna, 1794-1876.

Iron filigree work in the hacienda.

JALAPA

(Náhuatl: *xalli*, sand, *apan*, river)

The famous hinterland cities of Veracruz developed like the hill stations of India as a refuge from the yellow fever, cholera, malaria, and dysentery of the coast. The first sizeable settlement was Jalapa, which was already a thriving Indian community when Cortés marched through it in 1519, and is now the capital of the state. Like a colossal urban staircase, it connects the tropical valleys of the lowlands to the bleak, cold plain of Perote.

Halfway up, on a broad landing, is the administrative, cultural and commercial center of the city. There orchids grow on the trunks of the jacarandas near the stone balustrades of a small park, and there the mangoes, sapodillas, avocadoes and bananas from the tropical valley below climb up the steep streets to meet the plum, pear and apple trees descending from the temperate upper reaches of the town .

Tabasco. Jalapa. Exterior of the Museum of Anthropology.

This page and above left: Olmec and post-Olmec sculptures appear in a surf of greenery that flows gently along the sloping site of the museum.

Veracruz. El Tajín. The city flourished between 600 and 1000 A.D. with a prominent role in Mesoamerican civilization. This architectural complex is distinguished from other archeological sites by the coffered niches on the seven levels of its principal pyramid.

Top left: Panorama of the Plaza Arroyo.

Bottom left: North wall of the Pelota Court. Early classic Mayan.

Above: Pyramid of the Niches. One of the most elegant buildings in Mesoamerica.

99

In Yucatán, the past outweighs the present. In Veracruz, the scholars think of the past, the politicians of the future, but to the jarocho-in-the-street, the present is all. So let us here choose a guide closer to our own time, deserting the incomparable Bernal Diaz del Castillo for a tireless, curious and wickedly observant Scots woman who arrived in Veracruz in 1839.

Fanny Calderon de la Barca (née Frances Erskin Inglis) was the wife of Spain's first envoy to Mexico after Independence. She was possessed of a sharp tongue and a kind heart, and allowed ample scope to both in her journals and letters.

Few love affairs have begun as unpromisingly as Fanny's with Mexico. She hated Veracruz on sight. "Anything more melancholy, *délabré*, and forlorn than the whole appearance of things cannot be imagined. On one side the fort (San Juan de Ulua), with its black and red walls; on the other the miserable, black-looking city, with hordes of large black birds, called *zopilotes*, hovering over some dead carcass, or flying heavily along in search of carrion." The sand dunes described by Bernal grew in Fanny's eyes to "mountains of moving sand, formed by the violence of north winds." The cookery was "the worst of Spanish, Vera-crucified, but loads of it . . . garlic and oil enveloping meat, fish and fowl, with pimentos and plantains, with all kinds of curious nasty fruit which I cannot yet endure." She found the weather in December "very sultry," concluding that "this place which now seems like Purgatory must in summer, with the addition of the *vomito negro* (as they here call the yellow fever), be truly a chosen city!" Fanny's reactions may seem excessive but her descriptions were probably accurate. The unending civil wars and the plague had left Veracruz blackened and dilapidated.

Now, of course, Fanny's own name must head the list of those who succumbed to the enchantment of Veracruz. When she left the country two years later, she gave a glowing account of the building and heroic defense of San Juan de Ulua. And the food! "Veracruz cookery, which two years ago I thought detestable, now appears delicious to me! What excellent fish! – and what incomparable *frijoles* (beans)."

All the same, her first impression was understandable. The seaside approach to Veracruz discourages the traveler. The jungle of Eden, which Douanier Rousseau marched through with Napoleon III's troops and years later painted from memory, is in the hinterland. Fanny saw it a few days after her arrival, the thick leaves with pink spikes, the hidden monkeys and lurking tigers, when she and her husband visited General Santa Anna at his lush hacienda, Manga de Clavo. But its "beauty and fertility" could not hide the unhealthiness of the place. One look at the Santa Anna family told her all. "He is yellow, his wife and daughter are green."

The casual visitor cannot work up any interest in its provincialism, the early *paseo* around the plaza, the open-air social club for lovers and strolling musicians, for vendors of ices, lottery tickets, pastries, baby parrots and adult macaws, for jumping children and clusters of gas-filled balloons. The domino players, the beer and coffee drinkers, the café politicos, favor the marimba music of the arcaded *portales* around the square, while the floodlit City Hall transforms the plaza into a stage set.

From the time of its wholly imaginary but perfectly legal founding by Cortés, Veracruz has been the foremost port of Mexico. For more than a century it remained Europe's only door to the New World. Before long, Veracruz became Europe's door to the Orient as well. The Manila Galleon brought silks, porcelain, ivory and spices to Acapulco, whence the powerful merchant-shippers from Mexico City and Puebla sent them on to Spain through Veracruz. Thus the establishment of the overland Veracruz-Acapulco link finally provided the long-sought European route to the Orient.

In 1522, Cortés imported a lot of sugar cane from the Canary Islands and built an *ingenio* – a sugar mill – in the fertile hinterland of Veracruz. The industry prospered but the Indians collapsed. Negro slaves were brought in from the Caribbean islands. They survived in their new occupation and multiplied so rapidly that in 1602 they were strong enough to stage a rebellion and escape from their Spanish owners. In 1609, the Crown recognized the justice of their cause, granted them liberty and a tract of land where they founded the town of San Lorenzo de los Negros, now called Yanga after their original rebel leader.

The silver strike of the Zacatecas in 1548 made Veracruz the most tempting morsel for privateers in the New World. Millions in bullion were sometimes stored there, waiting to be picked up by the Spanish fleet. There were pirates of every nationality, but historical circumstances favored those who sought the protection of the English, Dutch or French sovereigns, Spain's traditional enemies. These were outraged at Pope Alexander VI's presumption in splitting the newly discovered lands of Africa, India and the New World between Spain and Portugal. It became a matter of honor to arm and license corsairs for the purpose of acquiring a share in the wealth of the New World. In New Spain, the cities of Campeche and Veracruz were main targets. The depredations of John Hawkins and Francis Drake in the 1570's and the Dutchman– Laurent de Graff, "Lorencillo" a century later, obliged Spain to build fortifications around these towns. The walls of Campeche are still standing, as are those of San Juan de Ulua, both equally useless.

CÒRDOBA

The rebellion of the Negro slaves was indirectly responsible for the founding of this charming town. The Negro rebels had become a menace to all traffic on the Mexico-Orizaba road, so a fort was built for the protection of wayfarers and was manned by thirty volunteers from Huatusco. In 1617 those same men founded Cordoba, which since has been known also as the City of the Thirty Cavaliers. Cordoba takes its aristocratic antecedents seriously and, fortunately, its rich farmlands have given it the means of living up to them. Yet in the end, it is the astonishingly varied beauty of Veracruz that seduces the traveler rather than the historical accomplishments of its inhabitants: the sheer drop from Acultzingo in the clouds to the intensely cultivated valley of Orizaba, the conical peak of Citlaltepetl reaching up to the stratosphere; the coffee plantations near Huatusco under a canopy of shade trees; the lagoon of Catemaco; the giant ficuses with saplings, vines and epiphyses springing from the crotches on the highest branches.

ORIZABA
(Náhuatl: *ilizapan*, joyful, *apan*, river.)

The snowy mantle of Mexico's highest (5,747 meters) and most symmetrical volcano, the peak of Orizaba, is the first landfall of a sea voyager bound for Veracruz. Fanny Calderon de la Barca saw it a full week before arriving in Veracruz. The Aztec name for it is Citlaltepetl, "Star Mountain," and the gleam of its snowcap on the darkest nights served as a beacon for wayfarers.

Spanish settlers were attracted by the excellent soil and climate, and soon populated the area after practically exterminating the Indian population. It quickly became a prosperous agricultural community. In 1873, the Mexico-Veracruz railroad passed through Orizaba, a recognition of its importance that also assured its long-term prosperity.

TLAXCALA

(Náhuatl: *Tlaxcalli*, tortilla, a maize pancake)

This is the smallest state in Mexico, carved out of the giant Intendancy of Puebla in 1793 by the second Viceroy Gálvez. In contrast to Veracruz, man and not nature has created Tlaxcala's most impressive monuments.

For modern Tlaxcala it has all been downhill since the eighteenth century. Despite its valiant efforts to keep abreast of the times, nothing in its recent history can match its pre-Hispanic political and military importance, nor the architectural splendor of its Colonial past. Fortunately, a suffi-cient number of buildings are still standing to attest to the latter, while a history of the former was written for us a few decades after the Conquest by Diego Muñoz Camargo, a Mestizo whose Tlaxcalan mother had lived through many of the events recorded by Bernal.

The earliest chroniclers called Tlaxcala a republic for lack of a better term for this unprecedented federation of independent seigneuries. Four states were involved, each rep-resented by a lord or elder. Three of the lordships were hereditary, the fourth was elective. Though women were excluded from voting, they could inherit lands and possess goods independently of their husbands. A polygamous but tightly knit family life was the foundation of Tlaxcala's stability, and men who remained unmarried after the age of twenty-seven suffered the indig-nity of having their hair cropped. Though trained in warfare since earliest youth, the Tlaxcalans were not unlettered Spartans.

Being ancestral enemies of the Aztecs, the Tlaxcalans helped Cortés build the boats with which he proposed to besiege the great city on the lake. The elder Xicoxtencatl – Don Lorenzo de Vargas since his baptism – gave Cortés the ten thousand warriors he requested, and offered as many more as he might need to carry the boats to the shores of Lake Texcoco.

After the Conquest, the Tlaxcalans followed Cortés on his voyages north and south and were instrumental in the colonization of New Spain and Central America. Pedro de Alvarado took his Tlaxcalan bride with him on the conquest of Guatemala, where she bore him the first Guatemalan Mestiza, Doña Leonor de Alvarado.

The grateful Cortés granted them special priv-ileges, later confirmed by the Crown. These included keeping their exclusively Indian gov-ernment, exemption from all tributes, the right to bear a coat of arms, to ride horseback, to be addressed as dons, and to work for their own benefit whatever mines they found, as well as the lands they already possessed and those that were later granted to them.

Cortés founded the city of Tlaxcala in 1520 on an uninhabited plain, in order not to impinge on the autonomy of the native seigneurs. When the Franciscans arrived in 1524, they agreed to divide their efforts into four missions: Churubusco, near Mexico City; Texcoco; Tlaxcala; and Huejotzingo. The establishment of the Franciscan convent in Tlaxcala began the building spree – no other word suggests the exuberance of the results – that turned Tlaxcala into a veritable treasure–house of ecclesiastical architecture. The friars imposed their Plateresque version of the Renaissance on the earliest buildings. The walls, the corner chapels, and the façade of the Convent of San Francisco, for example, reflect this classical austerity. As they began to work on the interiors, the Indian craftsmen, having mastered the technique of iron tools, became more exuberant. Their work grew elaborate in the gilded *retablos* (reredos) behind the altars, the turned grilles, and the airy Moorish style of the beamed and coffered ceilings. By the middle of the eighteenth century, both friars and native craftsmen were completely carried away. The Sanctuary of Ocotlán, on a hilltop outside the city, is an enchanting summary of their joyful art. Towers of spun sugar rest on bases faced with orange–pink tiles. The white shell façade juggles lightly with all the elements of the Baroque, and the traveler enters the church begging for more. The interior, rich as it is, comes as a disappointment after the breath–taking originality of the façade. Many turn back at this point, not knowing that the plum is hidden behind the main altar – the Virgin's Chamber, a tall octagonal well rising through carved gold to a jubilant vision of glory above. A single Indian craftsman by the name of Francisco Miguel carved it in the 1740's, possibly thinking that his scrolls, volutes, columns, and polychrome divines represented a realistic inventory of Heaven's furnishings. Whether accurate or just plain giddy, his vision continues to dazzle and astonish.

Tlaxcala Ocotlán. Above: the two white towers of the Basilica.

Opposite page: The gate to the Basilica of the Virgin of Opotlán, built in the 18th century, a monument of the Spanish Baroque.

Next page: Tlaxcala. An elaborate coffered ceiling of precious woods in the temple of San Francisco, 16th century.

"Woe is Mexico!" goes the saying. "So far from God, so close to the United States." Tlaxcala must have felt the same about the Spanish Crown and its local representatives.

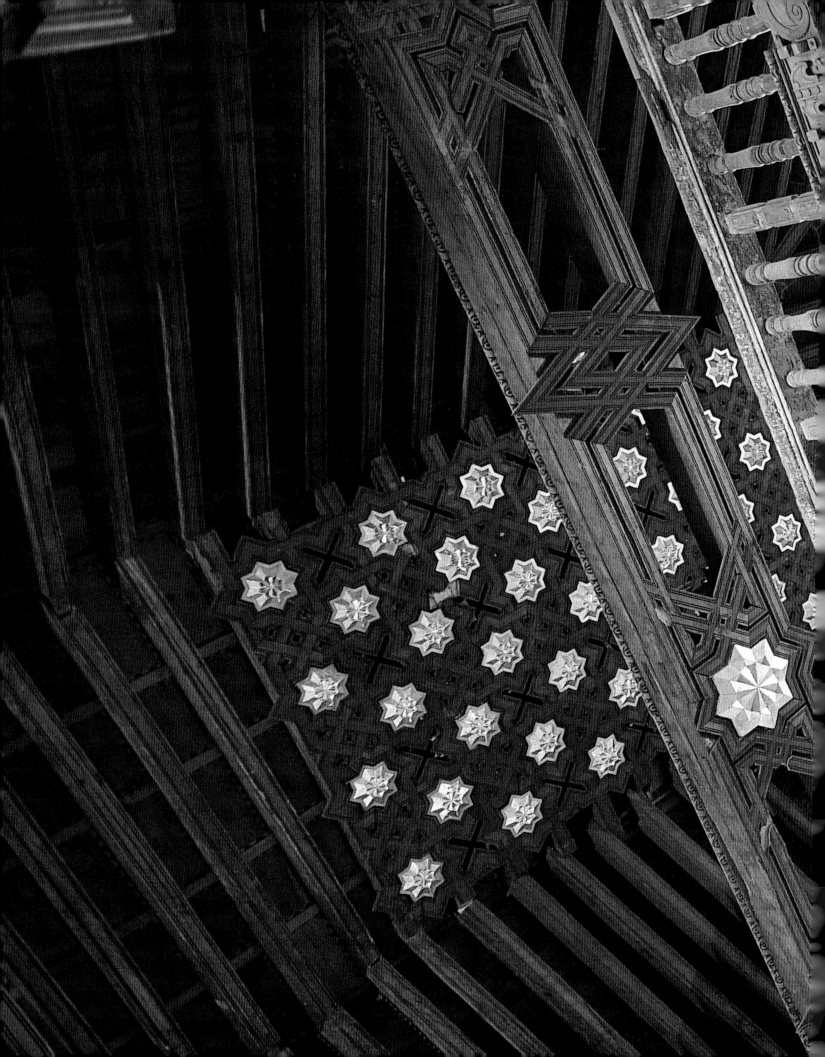

Puebla. A detail of Posa Chapel of San Francisco at the convent of Calpan, 16th century.

Opposite page: Puebla, the glorious embroidered interior of The Rosary Chapel in the Church of Santo Domingo. A Baroque gem, the walls are ensconced with ornate carvings, tiles and cherubs, all gilded.

"Si a morar en Indias fueres, que sea donde los volcanos vieres." If you go to live in the Indies, let it be where you can see the volcanoes." Did this piece of doggerel influence the choice of site for the city of Puebla de los Angelos? It is anyhow sound advice. Notice the plural "volcanoes," which refer unmistakably to Popocatépetl and Iztaccihuatl. The two volcanoes can only be seen simultaneously from the temperate valley of Puebla, Morelos and Mexico City itself, where the climate is more conducive to a long life.

In pre–Hispanic days, though fertile and well irrigated, the site where Puebla now stands was uninhabited. Like Veracruz, Puebla was a city created by fiat. Unlike Veracruz, however, it was not the result of a political coup, but of detailed planning. Sensing the social threat posed by the large floating population, the Second Audiencia decided to found a city for these displaced Spaniards. Puebla was officially established in 1531 and was paced out according to the traditional design of a Spanish city: a central square, presided over by the church and set in the middle of a grid of wide streets and square blocks. As an urban experiment it served the double purpose of settling the surplus population and protecting the route between Mexico City and Veracruz.

It flourished prodigiously. A few years later, the enthusiastic Franciscan Motolinía called it the second most beautiful city in New Spain. Though it first prospered as an agricultural community, industrial works and commerce soon changed the character of the town. *Obrajes* (textile mills), the first glassworks of Mexico, and shops displaying ceramics in the Talavera style so loved by Spaniards replaced the stables and orchards that had originally filled the city blocks. Presently the textile mills moved out to the countryside. In their place, nunneries, monasteries, and churches appeared, and the locally-produced tiles and bricks covered the façades of the larger houses, producing the colorful, even gaudy effect of the *poblano* style (the outstanding

Opposite page: Puebla. Main façade of the church and portal of the Convent of Huejotzingo. The delicate carved stone of the doorway belies the primitive simplicity of the fabric.

Puebla. Trumpeting angels announcing the Final Judgement in the Franciscan Temple of Huaquechula.

example being the House of Tiles – the original Sanborn's – in Mexico City).

Puebla's importance as a commercial crossroads, industrial center, and agricultural producer made it a coveted prize in every national and international struggle. The French suffered their greatest defeat there on 5 May 1862, in their first attempt to take the city. Though General Zaragoza was the Mexican commanding officer, the credit for the victory was given to the young General Porfirio Díaz (the future strong man) and won him a national following. And it was also in Puebla, on 20 November 1910, that Aquiles Serdan, his sister, Carmen, and his brother, Maximo, fired the first shots of the revolution that put an end to Díaz's thirty-year dictatorship.

The number of its religious establishments earned Puebla the reputation of being a dour and "Levitical" city. That is certainly the impression it made on Fanny Calderón de la Barca, who called Puebla "the Philadelphia of the republic," clean, well-paved and dull. "Its extreme cleanness after Mexico is remarkable…The ladies smoke more, or at least more openly, than in Mexico; but they have so few amusements they deserve more indulgence. There are eleven convents of nuns in the city, and taking the veil is as common as getting married."

Church of Guadalupe

Opposite page: Puebla. Church of San Francisco Acatepec. Indian Baroque tile and woodcarvings combining Christian and indigenous ideals.

Puebla. Church built on top of Tepanampa Pyramid in Cholula.

CHOLULA
(Náhuatl: *cholollan*, place of highwaymen)

Puebla. Cholula. The steps leading to the hilltop of the Sanctuary of Our Lady of Remedios, built in 1660.

Mexican schoolchildren are still told that Cholula has 365 churches – one for every day of the year– each built on the site of a pre-Hispanic temple. Few visitors who go there actually try to count. Those who do quit after the first ten or twenty; too much dusty walking is involved. So the myth persists, though after the holocaust and demolition of the *teocallis* by Cortés and his Tlaxcalan allies, only thirty-four churches finally went up, including the church built on the top of the giant pyramid which the Spaniards, despite all their efforts, were unable to destroy. This grafted–on Christianity never quite took, as though the fanaticism of both sides had rendered the soil sterile to further religious endeavors. Most of the churches are deserted, and Cholula is now merely a bubbly–domed architectural curiosity, the ghost of a once sacred city. Where Christianity was not so violently imposed, however, it found a soil as fertile as any in the New World. One of these places is Huejetzingo, the friendly town the Tlaxcalans recommended instead of the treach–erous Cholula. One of the four original Franciscan convents was founded there to take advantage of the large Indian population as a source of both labor and converts.

Puebla. The sanctuary in Cholula.

CHAPTER 3

Tierra
Caliente

*Morelos. The aqueduct of the sugar mill at Hacienda
Chiconcuac, established in the 16th century by the
Mexican Martín Cortés, son of the Conquistador.*

THE ISTHMUS OF TEHUANTEPEC

(Náhuatl: "the hill of the wild animal," from *tecuan*,
wild animal, and *tepec*, hill)

The Isthmus is considerably more than the narrowest part of the Mexican mainland. This strip of land represents the geographical divide between North and Central America. Its barriers of jungles, swamps, rivers, and mountains prevented any extensive mixing between the northern civilizations of Mesoamerica and the Maya of the south. After the Conquest, the centralist government of New Spain found itself cut off by the Isthmus from the dependencies of Yucatán, Guatemala, and Panama, which developed their own centers of government. Thus the Isthmus effectively isolated the area to the east and south of it from the mainstream of Mexico's development.

CHIAPAS

(Náhuatl: *chia-apan*, river of *chia*,
the Salvia Hispanica)

In pre-Hispanic times Chiapas formed an integral part of the Mayan civilization. Most local Indians are descended from the Maya, as are their languages and dialects. Chol, Tzeltal, Tzotzil, Tojolabal, and Zoque are a few of the local groups. The highland Indians, preponderantly Tzotzil and Tzeltal, are usually lumped together as Chamulas. They have maintained their vigorous individuality through the centuries. Their typical male costume consists of a black woolen poncho over a white smock (if single) or white britches (if married). It would look monkish except for the fringe of multicolored ribbons hanging from the rims of their flat straw hats. Their hilltop cemetery of San Juan Chamula is a place of poetry. A mound of earth marks each grave. An ordinary wooden cross stands at the head and a plank rests on the mound. But at the high, far end of the graveyard rises a Golgotha of gigantic wooden crosses, twenty to thirty feet high, painted in all colors – green, brown, purple, pink – bearing witness before the vivid sky.

*Opposite page:
Burial of
Huitzilihuitl the
Younger at
Chapultepec Hill.*

AN ELEGY FOR THE LACANDÓNES

"The Men of the Forest" Jacques Soustelle calls them in his excellent study, *The Four Suns*. They live in the rain and cloud forests between Mexico and Guatemala, a habitat Soustelle accurately describes as an "ocean of vegetation choked with water." The Lacandónes are the only Indians in Chiapas who speak anything like the classic Maya. Authorities agree that they originated in Yucatán, and are the descendants of those peasants who, a thousand years ago or more, left the great cities of the Maya to rot and collapse under their own weight. Soustelle visited six Lacandón *caribales* (hut clusters) and they accounted for nearly half of the total population of "perhaps two hundred Indians scattered over an area of nearly 39,000 square miles…" Soustelle's book recounts a trip he took to Lacandón country in the 'thirties. The 1976 *Enciclopedia de México* estimates that no more than 150 are left, though their numbers may have increased slightly in recent years.

"No structure can persist when society itself falls below a certain density," writes Soustelle. An agricultural people, the only technique they know is slash-and-burn, which forces them to periodic moves. They are totally self-supporting, growing their own food, and making their garments out of fibers they grow or pick wild. But planting their maize where mahogany, cedar and sapodilla once stood, and burning precious woods to heat their *torillas* or roast an occasional monkey or parrot, means that they are literally eating their forests up.

Soustelle places the blame of the Mayan decline squarely on the shoulders of the priestly mathematician, who kept raising taxes in order to finance the construction of ever more magnificent ceremonial centers, and to subsidize research into the nature and use of the zero and the positional value of numbers. These were achievements the peasants neither understood nor cared about. The men whose work sustained this admirable civilization wanted simpler gods, the kind found among trees, caves, and undefiled waters. Their kind seeped away into the forest where they took up the life of solitude and bare survival they still lead.

Watercolor by Nigel Hughes, 1986.

Chiapas. Palenque. In a tropical rain-forest,
a Mayan city which developed during the
first millennium A.D. and was one of the
most spectacular centers of the ancient world.
The temple is most famous because of the
rich treasure of jade found there.
The Temple of Inscription is on the left
and the palace on the right.

PALENQUE
(Maya-*Chol*: "stockade")

Soustelle describes this process with particular reference to Palenque. That city of grey and golden monuments died when it was "deprived of its labor force and food supply; it became a brain without a body and died of starvation. The elite caste itself was dispersed, the avenues disappeared under the advancing brush, and the first sprouts of the future jungle appeared on the steps of the pyramids and the roofs of the palaces." Palenque had been dead six hundred years when Cortés and his men marched unseeing past it on their ill-starred expedition to Las Hibueras in the south. Centuries would elapse before modern archeologists began a systematic study of the site. Sylvanus Morley, the dean of Mayan studies, considered Palenque the most beautiful ceremonial center in the Mayan world. The superbly delicate architecture set in a jungle raucous with monkeys and birds in brilliant flight is irresistible.

Palenque.
Detail of stele.

Diego de Mazariegos, arriving in 1526, was the first European to gain a foothold and establish Spain's dominion over the land. His decisive battle with the Chiapa Indians took place on a bluff high above the Sumidero canyon, a deep gully cut through the rock by the Grijalva River near Tuxtla. The gorge is dauntingly sheer, but rather than surrender to the Spaniards, the desperate and defeated Chiapas threw themselves into the abyss. The Spaniard, shocked, ordered his men to cease fire and made every effort to reassure the terrified survivors.

Mazariegos found a cool and pleasant valley above Chiapa de los Indios and there, in 1528, he founded a town which he named Villarreal. The First Audiencia changed the name to Villaviciosa; later it was generally known as San Cristóbal de los Llanos, and lasted until 1829, when it was renamed San Cristóbal de Las Casas, in honor of its first Bishop, Bartolomé de Las Casas.

Indians from Chiapas.

This militant Dominican is one of the most controversial figures in the history of New Spain. His lifelong mission was the protection of the Indians from the depredations of the Spaniards. He was as fearless as he was ruthless in pursuing his mission. His knowledge of his subject, however, was decidedly spotty. After Salamanca he had moved to the New World, where he acquired an *encomienda* on the island of Hispaniola. Revolted by the heartless exploitation of the natives, he returned to Spain in 1514, the year in which the Laws of Burgos, the Crown's earliest attempt to legislate in favor of the Indians, were enacted. He therefore witnessed only the first and worst period of Spanish colonization, but that became his immutable point of reference. He spent the rest of his life agitating and engaging in polemics while he traveled back and forth between the Old World and the New. Storming over the paper and sealing-wax hurdles of the Council of Indies, he gained the ear of Charles V and succeeded in pushing through the New Laws of 1542, which formally abolished the encomienda though it lingered on in other guises long after it had been declared officially dead.

Moral fervor being what it is, Fray Bartolomé soon had more enemies than friends. In Chiapas he was the first – and most hated – bishop. San Cristóbal was, after all, a town founded by and for *encomenderos*, and he left his see in fear of his life before a year was over. He returned to Spain to his writing and his disputations. Though he did not resign from his bishopric until 1550, he never returned to the New World.

His *Brief Relation of the Destruction of the Indies* made him a celebrity both in Europe and the New World. Rather than straight history, it is a denunciation of Spanish iniquity. Finally, even the seraphic Franciscan Fray Toribio Motolina lost patience with him and his incessant muckraking, and in 1555 wrote a famous letter to Charles V telling him so.

Fray Bartolomé presented his country and his Church in the worst possible light. Consequently, though regarded by most official historians as the protector of the Indians, the more independent of them look on him as the originator of the Black Legend regarding Spain.

The political development of Chiapas predictably resembles that of Yucatán, and for the same reason: its remoteness from Mexico's center of power. The citizens of both provinces considered themselves Yucatecos or Chiapanecos first, and Mexicans only by accident. Like Yucatán, Chiapas declared its independence from Mexico for a couple of years (1823–24). Its periodic Indian rebellions culminated, as in Yucatán, in a widespread genocidal War of Castes in 1868. Yet what reads like straight history in Yucatán can turn into slapstick in Chiapas, or degenerate into something unearthly and lurid. Thomas Gage, a young Dominican missionary, tells us about a "chocolate war" between the bishop and his flock that took place in San Cristóbal in 1626 or 1627. It all began because the ladies of San Cristóbal loved their chocolate and could not go without it even for the length of a Mass. "It was much used by them," writes Gage, "to make their maids bring them to church in the middle of Mass or sermon a cup of chocolate, which could not be done without great confusion and interrupting both Mass and sermon." The bishop cautioned them, the ladies ignored him. The following Sunday they found nailed to the cathedral door a threat of excommunication. "In that time the bishop fell dangerously sick. Physicians were sent for far and near, who all with joint opinion agreed that the bishop was poisoned." A prominent gentlewoman was commonly censured. She was said to have prescribed "such a cup of chocolate (to poison) him who so rigorously had forbidden chocolate to be drunk in the church."

The Chiapas War of the Castes took place in a world of the imagination where real blood was shed. A Chamula shepherdess one day found some "colored pebbles," which, she told her mother, "descended from heaven." The mother showed them to the headman of the village, who put them in a box and told everyone the following day that they had kept him awake all night long. They spoke to him, he said, they cried and beseeched him to take them out of the box. Such awesome news attracted a large public and the man founded a religious sect, declaring the shepherdess and another woman saints and burning incense before them. They bitterly felt the lack of their own Messiah, since, as they complained, the white man's Christ did not protect the Chamulas. So on Good Friday, 1868, before a gathering of several thousand Chamulas, the village chief, assisted by two female saints, crucified the shepherdess's younger brother. While some of the faithful drank the blood from his limbs and from the cross, the rest danced and sang in ecstasy. Government authorities viewed the affair in a more somber light. They considered it murder; the Chamulas countered that it was a religious service. Unimpressed, the authorities arrested the celebrants and the war began. Thirteen thousand Chamulas attacked the barrios of San Cristóbal. After many skirmishes and countless deaths on both sides, the Chamulas were finally defeated and their leaders shot in the central square. From there the soldiers fanned out through the countryside, hounding the Chamulas out of their hiding-places and slaughtering them in their own villages.

Such episodes leave the reader stunned with horror. Still, some questions remain. How did that shepherdess think up the bit about the colored pebbles descend from heaven? And what lead the Chamula chief to say they spoke to him and gave him instructions?

Historians dismiss these questions as pure local color witchery, yet anyone who has read R. Gordon Wasson's seminal studies on "entheogenic" ("God-within-us") mushrooms in Mesoamerica must immediately recognizer the colored pebbles as the magic mushrooms of mycolatry. Wasson found in the Bibliothèque Nationale in Paris a post-Conquest codex in which two men are shown speaking, their speech illustrated by black,

comma–shaped balloon–glyphs issuing from their mouths. Below them, line up in a row, are four mushroom caps with a glyph issuing from each one of them. The two men are apparently involved in a trial and, according to the inscription on the codex, are waiting to hear the mushrooms' opinion. The link between this tableau, the talking pebbles and the crucifixion of the Chamula boy seems clear.

The mushroom cult went underground with the advent of the Christian vine and wine culture, though in practice, as Wasson has shown, it continues to this day. There is ample documentary evidence to the effect that mushrooms and alcohol do not mix, either culturally or psychologically.

The Indian rebellion that began January 1, 1994 is a typical sequel to this history.

OAXACA

(Náhuatl: *Huaxyacac*, "where the gourds sprout" from *huaxi*, gourd, and *yacatl*, nose or tip, the beginning or end of something)

"Mexico is a western country by day and an Indian country at night." So said José Vasconcelos, a writer and politician of extravagant gifts who once dreamed of cleaning up the Revolution. His statement is perhaps truer of Oaxaca, his native state, than of Mexico in general. Spanning all history, glowing in dark places and observed respectfully only at night, the cult of the god-bearing mushroom weaves its thread through the life of the Oaxaqueños.

Oaxaca. Figurine of Iguana man.

DRUGS AND SACRIFICE

After his year of earthly pleasure and adoration, the godly youth ascends the pyramid to his sacrifice, breaking his flutes and dropping them on the steps. A maiden and her attendants dance towards the temple of the Maize God. As she steps across the threshold, the officiating priest decapitates her with a single stroke of his gold-handled flint knife. The surrogate of the Flayed God is gorgeously bedecked before being flayed alive by the priest who will then don his skin. The priests who sacrifice to Huitzilopochtli drink the victim's blood from his still-beating heart. The elegant serenity of the sacrificial victims is the dominant key of all the accounts of human sacrifice that have reached us. More than *sangfroid*, it amounts to a collaboration which mere respect for the ceremonial cannot sufficiently explain. In the ceremonial ball game, the captains of both teams were sacrificed, the loser for his unworthiness, the winner for his excellence. Yet knowing that death was the prize, both played as if to save their lives – or their honor.

The most likely explanation for all this lies in the drug culture of the pre-Hispanic Indian civilizations. Respect for ritual honor alone seems superhuman under the circumstances. Since alcohol inspires no such *beaux gestes*, only the special influence of a drug would seem to give that kind of sustaining power.

BEFORE CORTÉS: MONTE ALBÁN

In the 1930's the archeologist Alfonso Caso explored a burial mound in Monte Albán, and there found a treasure of gold and silver jewelry, quartz vessels, jade, and turquoise mosaics. The rich find in the middle of the Great Depression captured the world's imagination. Suddenly everyone wanted to know more about Monte Albán, about the Zapotecs who built it, and about the Mixtecs who made the exquisite articulated jewelry. Oaxaca experienced the first of its tourist booms in the twentieth century.

As with practically everything in Mesoamerica, Monte Albán began with the Olmecs. Two thousand years before Cortés, some Olmec groups left their steamy jungles on the Gulf coast and came to settle in the central valley of Oaxaca, a brisk 1,500 meters above sea level. They left massive foundations on Monte Albán, on which the Zapotecs later built their temples. The Monte Albán civilization, together with Teotihuacán and the classic Maya, dominated the entire classical period, our first millennium. All three were theocracies, ruled by a caste of astronomer-priests. Teotihuacán was the most influential, trading far and near throughout Mesoamerica and beyond it. The Maya were the most advanced mathematicians. Monte Albán's eminence, however, was and is literally physical: the astronomer-priests leveled a mountain-top in the middle of the high Oaxaca valley in order to build their ceremonial center closer to the stars. The Mixtec name for Monte Albán, *Sahandevui*, means "at the foot of heaven."

The rectangular plaza is precisely oriented on the four points of the compass. The proportions of its surrounding structures, the alternating rhythms of staircases and entablatures, satisfy the most demanding criteria of classical harmony and equilibrium. A cosmic silence fills these heights. The astronomer-priests make their ghostly presence felt whenever they keep their appointments with the stars. In the last moon before the spring equinox, for example, a visitor standing on the southern platform looking north receives a clear sign from them at the end of the day. As the sun sets on his left, a full moon rises above the rim of the valley to the right. For an instant, the heavenly bodies hang in a perfect balance of the celestial mechanics, until the seesaw tilts to the west and the sun disappears in a horizon of liquid gold, leaving Monte Albán to receive the full silver flood of the moon.

The withering away of the classic civilizations toward the end of the first millennium left a power vacuum which produced a period of warring states. The theocracies of the Classic period were supplanted by the militaristic soci-

Oaxaca. Detail of the Basilica of the
Three Naves at Santiago Cuilapan.

Opposite page: Oaxaca. Open Chapel of
the Convent of Teposcolula, 16th century.

eties of the post-Classic. The Toltec-Chichimecs in central Mexico, and later in Yucatán, filled the spaces left by the Teotihuácanos and the Classic Maya. In the Oaxaca valley, the Mixtecs, longtime neighbors and allies of the Cholula Toltecs, emerged as the dominant people. They subjugated most of the Zapotec cities. Though some intermarriage took place between the princely families, they arrived definitely as conquerors, driving the more recalcitrant lordlings out of the valley toward the coast of Tehuantepec.

Oaxaca. Tlacochayoya, the organ in the church, 18th century.

Both Zapotecs and Mixtecs call themselves "the Cloud People," which suggests a common origin in the cloud forest of Oaxaca's northern mountains. The Zapotecs were evidently the first to populate the valley. During the prime of Monte Albán, the Mixtecs were still slashing and burning down their primeval cloud forests. The gradual erosion of their land finally forced them down to the valley as well. By the time they got to Monte Albán, it was already an abandoned graveyard, and as such they continued to use it, borrowing their predecessors' splendor for their own dead.

THE MARQUESS OF THE VALLEY OF OAXACA

Oaxaca is the phoenix of Mesoamerican cities, rising from its ashes after every holocaust. First razed by Moctezuma I in 1468, it was replaced by an Aztec fort that was again burned to the ground by the Spaniards in 1521. Some Spanish officers engaged in a coastal campaign against the Mixtecs found the site so attractive that they abandoned their garrison and founded a town where the fort had been. Cortés, infuriated, ordered the town to be dismantled and evacuated, and the founders to be brought back in chains. He wanted the valley of Oaxaca for himself.

The reason was gold. He was evidently acquainted with the Aztec tax rolls and coveted the wealth of the province. Cochineal (the royal purple dye), cacao, and quetzal feathers probably seemed small change to him; they only began to interest him after the dye and the chocolate drink became the rage in Europe. Cortés distributed encomiendas in the valley among his illegitimate children and his closest friends. But a royal order arrived in 1526 ordering the site of Oaxaca to be divided into building lots. Cortés intercepted the order and routed the presumptive settlers for the third time. The following year he personally took possession of the valley and planted the first fields of wheat. During his absence in Spain in 1528, Charles V's city charter was made effective, and a Spanish city was founded with the name of Antequera. In the same year the first Dominican missionaries arrived. Thus, when Charles granted Cortés the title of Marquess of the Valley of Oaxaca in 1529 and named him Captain General of New Spain, Cortés returned in triumph but found that the city of Oaxaca–Antequera had been placed forever beyond his reach.

The Spanish Crown granted many encomiendas and titles to the conquistadors of the New World. Cortés's title specifically included "the lands and vassals, the woods and pastures, all waters, both running and standing, and complete civil an criminal jurisdiction – all the rights in short, which belonged to the Crown itself in the aforesaid lands." Both Spaniards and Indians were included among his vassals, though only the latter owed him tribute.

MITLA

The Mixtecs settled in the Oaxaca valley about the year 1280, forty-one years before the Mexicas first arrived in Chapultepec. Mitla survived the Christian holocaust because it was not a ceremonial center but a complex of courts and palaces built by the Mixtecs in the vicinity of some Zapotec temples. From a distance it looks like a squat convent with some very ordinary cupolas and a sawed-off bell tower. Drawing closer, its post-Classic character becomes aggressively evident: the sides of the building jut out, like a section of a pyramid placed upside down.

The domes, it turns out, belong to a primitive Christian church behind the compound. The proportions of the low, long facades recall some of the secular buildings of the Classic Maya in Yucatán. The decorative detail, however, is unimaginably complex, like a sampler embroidered by an obsessively cubistic nun. Mitla is a jigsaw puzzle – the ultimate jigsaw puzzle. Thousands of little stone bricks are tightly and precisely fitted into geometrical patterns running like lightning along the horizontal friezes. It is the apotheosis of zigzag.

Oaxaca. A 16th century church behind the Mitla ruins built by the Mixtec Indians. The buildings in Mitla are decorated with mosaic-stone patterns.

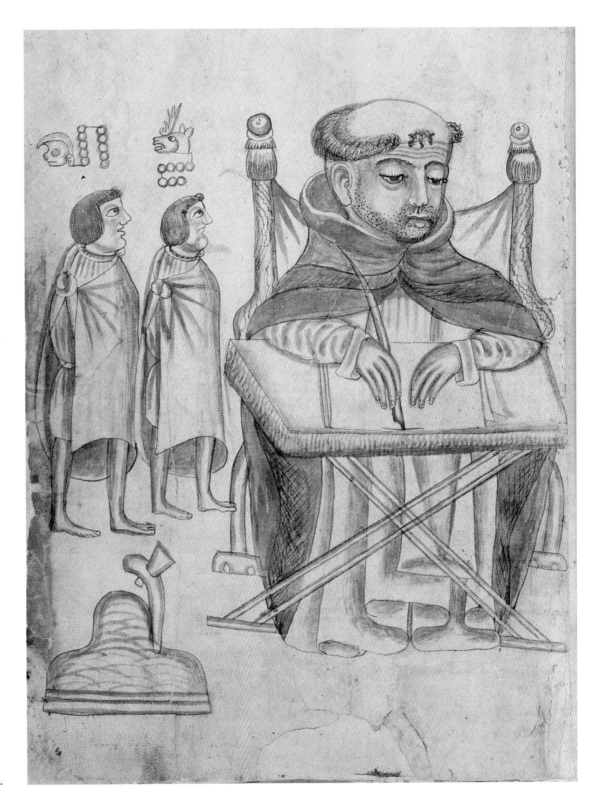

Oaxaca. Yanhuitlan Codex, 16th century. A friar records Indian traditions dictated by native lords behind him.

THE AZTEC INVASION

Between 1440 and 1470 the Aztecs from the war-like north finally ventured into the unyielding south. They were not at first strong enough to gain control of the Oaxaca valley, but sufficiently so to open lucrative trade routes to the cacao-rich lowlands of Tabasco and Chiapas. The cacao bean, after all, continued to be the accepted currency throughout Mesoamerica. A grandson of Moctezuma II, Fernando Alvarado Tezozomoc, wrote an account of the Aztec experience in Oaxaca in his *Crónica Mexicana* of 1598. On this occasion the inhabitant of Huazyácac captured and slaughtered a caravan of Aztec merchants and robbed them of their merchandise. Moctezuma I sent a punitive expedition to raze the town and some years later, in 1486, Ahuízotl built a fort there in its place. This was the beginning of what became in effect the Aztec occupation of Oaxaca.

When Cortés's first emissaries arrived in 1520, they found among the Oaxaca Indians many ready allies against the Aztecs.

DOMINICANS AND INDIANS: CONVENTS AND COMMUNITIES

The Dominican Order was the first of the Mendicant Orders to establish itself in Oaxaca. It was instrumental in achieving for the first time a degree of political unity in the province, first by mediating between Spaniards and natives, and then by intervening among the Indians themselves, isolated as they were by their mutually incomprehensible dialects and their multitude of villages, each fiercely individualistic and jealous of its rights. Their early involvement in this basic problem made the Dominicans the dominant religious order in Oaxaca.

Most of the natives quickly accepted Christianity; only the priestly élite fought back. The Dominicans adopted as many of the local customs, beliefs and rituals as they could in order to make conversion easier for the Indians. The old gods were turned into Christian saints. Cocijo, the Zapotec rain god, was translated into Saint Peter, who manages rainfall for Christians. A Zapotec heroine, Pinopiaa, was worshiped at the same shrine as Saint Catherine of Siena.

The converted masses broke the Dominicans' missionary hearts by getting gloriously drunk at every festival. The Indians' weakness for alcohol undoubtedly accounts for the harsh pre-Hispanic laws against drunkenness. Only the threat of capital punishment could keep them on the wagon. The Indians worked very hard, though, for their spiritual guardians. The Dominicans, not having taken a vow of poverty like the Franciscans, undertook commercial ventures and were able to build rich cloisters for themselves and even richer churches for God. The Convent of Santo Domingo in Oaxaca is probably the finest example of Dominican architecture in Mexico. Building was begun "with a few pennies" in 1547. The cloister, which now houses the Mixtec treasures of Monte Albán, was finished in the following century. In 1659 the monks brought in a stucco artist from Puebla to decorate the vaults and walls of the church. He designed a tree, and a bower and vine whose tendrils of green and gold entwine the heads of cherubs, saints, and Dominican precursors and missionaries, and present a synopsis of the Dominican order told in exuberant rococo against a dazzling background.

In Oaxaca land has always been the bone of contention. The pre-Hispanic villages had their communal lands. After the Conquest, the Crown had respected these *comunidades* based on their "primitive patrimony," and created further communal grants for the benefit of landless pueblos. The Indian thus became rooted to his soil and his immediate community. Though Spanish soon emerged as the *lingua franca* of the region owing to the multitude of dialects, the Indian languages continued to be spoken with undiminished vigor. They have reinforced the ancient community loyalties, leaving little or no room for broader ethnic or national sympathies .

State of Guerrero: Acapulco
(Náhuatl: *acatl*, reed, *pul*, augmentative particle, *co*,
locative ending, "place of thick reeds.")

Guerrero.
Map of Acapulco,
17th century. By
Adriaan Boot.

Spoiled or not, Acapulco continues to be Mexico's favorite resort. Hordes of honeymooners and holiday-makers rush lemming-like to Acapulco. They crowd onto beaches, sleeping on the sand, in campers, rooming houses or shoddy-expensive hotels. The real Acapulco, the one that has fabricated for itself a mystique of matchless hedonism throughout the world, the honeymooners do not even get a whiff of. It hovers in the blue air at an altitude of between 150 and 1000 feet above sea level, an altitude determined by the height of the most expensive penthouses and the villas with the grandest views. This Acapulco can only be reached on the big-money elevator or, if you are young, on the updrafts of warm and fragrant air that only beauty can generate.

Though Acapulco is no country for old men, the placed is packed with them. They have found there a Fountain of Youth. The old have the power, the young have the beauty: the two come together as inevitably as sex and money. The fountain jets play wherever the party is happening. This is a continuous, free-floating event moving from villa to penthouse and back.

Art and artifice can recreate some part of what the crowds and the higgledly-piggledy builders have spoiled. Without that kind of money, though, only a devotee of dawn and high purlieus may still catch a glimpse of Acapulco's fabled beauty.

THE ASIA ROUTE

Acapulco's present vogue has obscured its historical importance. Forty years after the Conquest, it became the Spanish Empire's gateway to the Orient and to its South American colonies. The discovery by Fray Andrés de Urdaneta of the safe and easy return route from the Philippines marked the beginning of the China trade. The Manila Galleon connected the Spanish merchants of Seville with the Spice Islands (the Moluccas). The footpath connecting Mexico City and Puebla with Acapulco came to be known as the Asia Route, and the Puebla merchants dealing with both Veracruz and Acapulco, as the *Mercaderes de Ambos Mares*, Merchants of Both Seas.

The market that took place in Acapulco in January, after the arrival of the Manila Galleon, became famous the "The Trade Fair of America," since it supplied the markets of Guatemala, Panama, Peru and Chile as well as those of Spain and New Spain. Acapulco became a babel during the fair. The Creole and Spanish merchants could not have understood a word said by the Japanese, Hindu, Malaysian and Chinese traders. The atmosphere of the port became as exotic as the silks, ivories, porcelains and spices that were its stock in trade. The fair generally ended up with a mock funeral that signaled the beginning of the pre-Lenten carnival celebration.

Inevitably, the freebooters arrived. The Dutch and English pirates who plagued the cities of the Spanish Main now turned their attention to the Pacific coast. In 1615 six vessels belonging to the Dutch east India Company entered the bay, though at the first cannon shots from land, the commanding officer hoisted the white flag. They exchanged their Spanish prisoners for fresh provisions. The experience led to the construction of the Fort of San Diego which, with substantial later modifications, still stands.

Painted folding screen, 1780.
Just as the merchandising activities of the English and the Dutch East India Companies sparked the fashion for things oriental in Europe — tulips, China ware, Indian printed cloths — the Manila Galleon brought its own chinoiserie to Mexico. Screens from China, Japan and the Indian coast of Coromandel were shipped to Acapulco but never arrived whole. They were too frail to survive the hazardous journey. So the logical solution was adopted: the makers of the screens were brought to Mexico. They were mostly Japanese, settling in the vicinity of Lake Pátzcuaro in Michoacán, where, in time, they took Mexican surnames and raised Mexican families to whom they passed on their expertise in lacquer. This eventually extended from the sumptuous colonial screens to humbler but more immediate necessities like wooden bowls and other household objects known as jaicaras, decorated with brilliantly-colored designs on a black lacquered ground.

Guerrero. Taxco. One of the twin bell towers of the Baroque Church of Santa Prisca, influenced by the chinoiseries introduced by the China trade.

TASCO

(Náhuatl: *Tlachco*") (in) the ball game")

The Asia Route was no more than a footpath negotiable only by the Indian *tamemes* (porters) until 1592, when the Viceroy Luis de Velasco II made it suitable for pack mules. During the dry winter months, the trip took twelve days; during the summer rains, traffic came to a standstill. Nothing more was done about the road until 1750, when a silver millionaire by the name of José de la Borda improved the stretch between Taxco and Cuernavaca.

The Taxco mines – tin and iron as well as gold and silver – had been continuously exploited since pre–Hispanic times. The big silver strikes occurred in the 18th century and the lode found by José de la Borda was one of the richest. When he broadened and repaired the road to Cuernavaca, he was at the peak of his pros–perity. His fortune was such that he also under–took the reconstruction of the ruined parish church of Santa Prisca, the crisp and fancifully elegant church with its bell towers like pagodas, which for many now stands as the perfect example of the Mexican Churrigueresque.

The gleam of silver shines throughout the history of Taxco. A school of silversmiths devel–oped that made Taxco a household word throughout Spain. Santa Prisca's silver treasure was particularly sumptuous. Most of it did not belong to the church, however. The canny Borda had only lent it to the parish, keeping the chalice, crowns, and candelabra as security against a rainy day. When his first mine gave out, and his first fortune came to an end, he still had these objects in reserve. A single mon–strance sold to Mexico City Cathedral fetched 110,000 pesos in 1762. With that, and a lucky strike into the *Veta Grande* (Mother Lode) of Zacatecas, he was able to restore his fortune. He died in Cuernavaca, a rich man, in the gardens he had built for his retirement and which still bears his name.

This state lies on the sun–washed southern slope of the Valley of Mexico. A countryside of gradually descending valleys, of rich soils and deep ravines, and a vegetation that luxuriates in its perpetual spring. Even the names of its two principal cities, Cuernavaca and Cuautla, reflect the *luxe, calme et volupté* of the climate and the vegetation. Cuautla, from the Náhuatl, *cuahuitl*, tree, with the collective *-tla* ending, means a woodland. Cuernavaca is merely the Spaniard's *cuerno y vaca* ("horn and cow"), a corruption of Cuauhnáhuac (near the Trees).

Morelos became an independent federal state in 1869. It was named after José Maria Morelos, the octoroon priest who became the leader of the Insurgency after the execution of Miguel Hidalgo. His audacious breakout from Cuautla, when it was besieged by the Royalist army, was a crucial triumph in the War of Independence. A child of the Enlightenment – he called himself "the bondslave of the nation" – he convoked the First Constitutional Assembly in Chilpancingo in 1813. The egalitarian, republican manifesto issued the following year declared the sovereignty of all the people; "*No Creoles or Castes,*" Morelos had said, "we are all Americans." This document is considered the forerunner of all our subsequent constitutions.

Like Miguel Hidalgo, Morelos was finally captured, tried, defrocked, and shot. In 1865 Maximilian, seduced by the exotic nature of Cuernavaca, took over the dilapidated Borda gardens and endeavored to restore them to their original splendor. Maximilian raised a statue in honor of Morelos fifty years after his execution, and only one year before he himself had to face Juárez's firing squad.

Morelos.
View of the volcano
Popocatepeti rising
behind an aqueduct.

As recently as 1930 Cuernavaca was still the town in which the rich built their pleasure domes, while Acapulco, long fallen from the bustle of its Manila Galleon days, remained a huddle of quite remarkable indistinctness. Now, of course, Acapulco has soared to the heights of tourist fame while Cuernavaca has become practically a suburb of Mexico City.

In pre-Hispanic times the population runoff from the valley – the late-comers, the weak, the unsuccessful – always spilled over toward the south and settled in the mild verdant region under the volcano. But a good climate and luxuriant vegetation also attract the powerful, and the warlords duly arrived, subdued the locals, and exacted tribute from them. Many tribes suc-ceeded one another in this fashion. A venerable Toltec legend relates that when the god Quetzalcóatl forsook eternity in order to enter worldly time, the incarnation took place in a virgin's womb and his birth as man took place in a valley to the east of Cuernavaca. The Aztec emperor Ahuízotl built the Tepozteco temple in his honor, on a cliff above the valley of Tepoztlán.

Cortés first became aware of these valley cultures in 1521, preparing for the siege of Tenochitlán. He had sent an expedition to identify the Aztec cities immediately to the south. When it returned badly mauled, he personally headed a second expedition, unexpectedly approaching Cuernavaca from the southeast, which the natives had considered sufficiently

Morelos.
Cuernavaca. View of
the Cathedral.

Hernan Cortés, the Conqueror, 1521.

Below: Morelos. The open cloister of the Cathedral de la Asunción, begun in 1526 in Cuernavaca.

Morelos. Church of the Capilla del Terzer Orden and a detail of the interior.

Morelos.
At the Hacienda
Chiconcuac, dating
from Martín Cortés,
flowering vines spill
over the stream.

Don José de la Borda, oil painting by Miguel Cabrera.

protected by natural obstacles. The ravine of Amanalco cut Cortés off from the fortified city of Cuauhnáhuac like a moat. The city seemed unassailable until his Tlaxcalan allies found an *amate* tree, an immense wild ficus whose great boughs overhung the ravine, allowing them to drop safely on the far side .

The Cuernavaca Municipal Codex relates that the natives, seeing the strange armored men approaching from the direction of the supposedly unbridgeable *barranca*, took fright and fled north. Leaving a detachment in charge, Cortés returned to Lake Texcoco and launched the siege that ended with the downfall of Tenochtitlán. He left the valley on 5 April 1521, took Cuernavaca on 13 April and Tenochtitlán four months later.

When Cortés received the title of Marquess of the Valley of Oaxaca in 1529, he made Cuernavaca the capital city of his fief. He had already built himself a palace there – the same which now houses a museum, and has some excellent murals, including *trompe l'oeil* furniture, by Diego Rivera. Cortés's second wife spent most of her time there. She was a peninsular aristocrat of unimpeachable lineage, and she preferred the sunny loggia overlooking the valley to the cold Coyoacán mansion where the Conquistador's first wife had died of poisoning. Cortés was accused of her murder and stood trial. The Court, the Second Audiencia (the good one) and even the dead woman's mother, ended up by agreeing that the charge was groundless.

Since 1523 Cortés had successfully grown sugar cane in the valley. His son, Martín, continued producing sugar after the conquistador's death. The report of stupendous profits attracted many Spaniards, but, as most of the land in the region belonged to the Marquesado and the convent it had endowed, the newcomers had to lease or buy from the Crown. They had no way to expand other than by "buying" or otherwise encroaching on the Indian communities' lands, which were inalienable by law. Later, the Reform Laws of 1857 legalized the purchase of these lands, which played straight into the *hacendados'* hands and left the communities destitute. Some growers even ploughed up the village streets to plant cane for their mills. The villagers had scant recourse to law, and in any case, could not expect to find a sympathetic ear with the state government, since it was hand-picked by Díaz from among his *hacendado* friends.

Morelos.
Cuernavaca. Above:
Boathouse at the
Borda garden.
Below: 18th century
fountain in the
same garden.

Morelos. Cuernavaca. Detail of Emiliano Zapata from Diego Rivera's mural "The History of Cuernavaca and Morelos" in the Cortés Palace, 1929-30.

Opposite Page Detail from the same mural "Crossing the Barranca".

EMILIANO ZAPATA (1879–1919)

Such were the conditions in which Emiliano Zapata grew up. Anencuilco, his native village, was one of those whose streets had been ploughed up for sugar cane. By 1900 most Indian communities found themselves without a scrap of land in which to plant their maize. When apprised of this situation, one hacendado suggested that they plant it in flowerpots. What followed was a revolution which permanently overthrew the landed aristocracy and deprived it of political power.

Zapata's open rebelliousness landed him in the army. There, his superb horsemanship caught the eye of President Díaz's son-in-law, who gave him a job looking after his thoroughbreds. After a few months Zapata returned to Anencuilco, where the community elected him president and entrusted him with the defense and recovery of their lands, whose titles dated from pre-Hispanic times and had been ratified by the Spanish Crown.

When the Revolution broke out, Zapata threw in his lot with Madero, insisting on the inclusion of a plank on agrarian reform in Madero's platform, which was a purely political one of "effective suffrage and no re-election." In the skirmishes, guerilla raids, and head-on battles of the Revolution, Zapata proved invincible. A total identification of purpose with the Indians and

dispossessed peasants of Morelos gave him a strength beyond numbers and logistics. He became a force of nature, cutting through the sectarianism that finally destroyed Madero's Revolution. His virtuosity on horseback earned him the name of "the Centaur of the South" even as Pancho Villa came to be known as "the Centaur of the North." Obsessed by the need for agrarian reforms, he quarreled with every revolutionary leader. After breaking with the Constitutionalist President Carranza, Zapata and Pancho Villa took Mexico City.

Detail of Zapata with a harvest of maize from Diego Rivera's mural "The Blood of the Revolutionary Martyrs Fertilizing the Earth". Autonomous University of Chapingo.

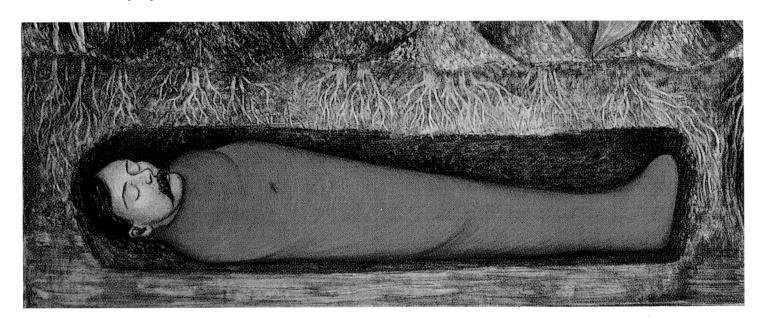

The terrified citizenry barricaded itself against "Attila's hordes." Nothing happened. Indians in coarse white drawers and enormous peaked hats wandered shyly around the city, still carrying their guns but meekly asking for directions. They disappeared as quietly as they arrived.

Finding Zapata invincible in the field, Carranza sent him a Trojan Horse, a fake defector from the Constitutionalist army. Laboriously, he earned Zapata's trust, taking government garrisons and even executing hostages. One day he invited Zapata to have lunch with him. Zapata arrived with a small escort at the defector's hacienda headquarters. The buglers greeted him with fanfares, a guard of honor presented arms. As the last note sounded, the guards shouldered their muskets and fired pointblank into Zapata's chest. Zapata's death has saved all subsequent agrarian leaders and governments a lot of embarrassment. In his name, politicians have transformed his ideal into an inexhaustible honey-pot.

Only one monument does Zapata justice: the effigy Rivera painted on the chapel walls of the former Hacienda of Chapingo, now the National School of Agriculture. There the dead crusader lies, in a coffin hollowed out of the earth, wrapped in the blood-stained shroud of a murdered man. The roots of the field are growing down through the earth into his niche to tap his strength. Zapata slumbers in the earth he loved, beyond the injustice he abhorred .

Morelos. Tepoztlán, view over the valley with the Dominican Convent.

CHAPTER 4

The Heartland: El Centro

View of the city of Zacatecas by Manuel Pastrana.

Mexico. Convent of Zinacatepec. Detail of genealogical tree of Franciscan Order, 16th century.

THE STATES OF MEXICO, HIDALGO, QUERÉTARO, GUANAJUATO, ZACATECAS, AGUASCALIENTES, DURANGO, SAN LUIS POTOSI, MICHOACAN, COLIMA, JALISCO, NAYARIT

These states comprise the quintessential Mexico, with its double-rooted past and its present coat of many colors. By comparison, the south seems too idiosyncratic, too close to its non–Mexican, pre–Hispanic roots, while the north is too rootless, too prone to veer away into the irresistible orbit of the United States.

In this central region we find the living reality of our three cultures. Native populations live in their original communities, and in countless country markets you are likely to hear as much Otomí and Náhuatl as Spanish. The Creoles have also traditionally gravitated toward certain regions like *los altos* (the highlands) of Jalisco where their high coloring and fair complexion emphasize their European features. And throughout one finds the Mestizos, the most numerous group in the country, the ones who, in the final analysis, keep Mexico more or less fueled and in working order.

In no other region can we find a richer and more varied collection of pre–Hispanic and Spanish Colonial monuments. The heartland illustrates the continuity of our pre–Hispanic culture, on the one hand, and , on the other, the wild variety of colonial invention which has resulted from the mixture of Spanish and Indian sensibilities. Geographically, it resembles the landlocked provinces of central Spain: wide, tawny plains, valley clenched in mountains and watered by the head streams that flow down to irrigate the pains along either coast. The churches with their cupolas, the fortress convents and the fortified *haciendas* scattered about the arid land–scape intensify the Castillian atmosphere. The cities San Miguel de Allende, Querétaro, Zasacatecas, and Morelia would not look out of place in Castile or Aragón .

The heartland also provides a summary of Mexican history. Our economy was forged in its

Mexico. Tepotzotlán. Interior of the former monastery, now the National Museum of the Viceroys.

151

Mexico. Toluca. Exterior of "Cosmovitral", the Botanical Garden, that used to be the marketplace where ceiling and walls were replaced by a stained glass version of the cosmos.

mines and haciendas. Our religion was carried to the farthest marches of the land, first by Spanish missionaries, then by their Indian and Mestizo disciples. The independent republic was born here, midwifed by Creole intellectuals and officers of the royalist army. The heartland cities held out against the French invasion and Maximilian's empire. Both Querétaro and San Luis Potosí were at one time or another capitals of the embattled republic.

To the north of Tenochtitlán extended the enormous territory of the *Gran Chichimeca*, a country occupied by tribes of nomadic hunters. To the west, the *Cultura de Occidente* fanned out to the Pacific coast, covering the present states of Michoacán, Colima, Jalisco, Nayarit, and snippets of all the states around them. The outlanders living closest to Tenochtitlán were the most civilized: the Otomics of Otumba, immediately north on the border of the Gran Chichimeca; and the Tarascan Kingdom of Michoacán directly to the west, which forms part of the Cultura de Occidente. The Indians of the more remote regions were the most indomitable. It took the forty-year Chichimeca War to subdue the

Guachichiles of San Luis Potosí, while the even more remote Coras of the Sierra in Nayarit were still unsubdued a hundred years ago.

The Gran Chichimeca

Once the Aztec Empire was sufficiently under control, Cortés, helped by his old and new allies, turned his attention to the north. The Franciscans were his most effective troops. They presently learned as much as any foreigner could about the local cultures. Some became linguists, like Fray Alonso de Molina, who wrote the first Náhuatl-Spanish dictionary. Another, Fray Francisco de Tembleque, turned out to be an architectural genius. Seeing the natives of Otumba drinking out of the same stagnant pools as the *encomendor's* horses and cattle, he conceived the idea of bringing fresh water in from Zempoala, 45 kilometers away, an awesome project on such broken terrain. With the help of several thousand Indians, and no technical knowledge beyond his common sense and intuition, he finished the work in seventeen years.

STATE OF MEXICO

(Náhuatl, *Mexictli*, "In the navel of the moon,"
from *metzli*, moon, and *xictli*, navel)

Since Classic times central Mexico has undoubtedly been the premier province of the country. On
its soil grew three of the sovereign civilizations of
Mesoamerica, the Teotihuacán, the Toltec, and
the Aztec, each supremely powerful in its own
day. The Aztec civilization looms larger than the
others because it is closer to us in time, and
because the Spanish Conquest caught and preserved it in the apogee of its power and splendor.
There is little reason to believe, though, that it was
in any way superior to those that preceded it.

After the 1824 Constitution, the State of Mexico
reflected the chaotic conditions of the country
as a whole. During the centralist interregnum of
1835-46, the State of Mexico became a department which included the Federal District and the
former State of Tlaxcala. With the restoration of
federalism in 1846, all the states went back to
their former boundaries. But three years later,
after the American war, the State of Mexico lost a
great deal of its territory with the creation of the
State of Guerrero, which extended practically
from Cuernavaca to Acapulco. During a brief
return to centralism in 1853, the "district" of
Morelos was organized within the revived
Department of Mexico. Then, during the French
Intervention, the State of Mexico was split up
into three military districts, which in 1869, after
the restoration of the republic, turned into the
separate states of Mexico, Hidalgo, and Morelos.

The State of Mexico, then, reduced from its
former exalted situation, suddenly found itself in
possession of some of the poorest soil but many
of the finest monuments, both pre-Hispanic
and of the old colonial Intendancy. This woeful
tale of mutilation, however, ends unexpectedly

Miguel Hidalgo y Costilla, detail of a mural by José Clemente Orozco, 1937.

Quetzalcóatl was generally identified with the morning star while his evening twin was transmogrified into a dog–headed god known as Xólotl. Xólotl was also the name for the Pame–Chichimec chieftain who ultimately destroyed Tula, the city that had expelled Quezalcóatl. This earthly Xólotl (1244–1304) achieved great power. He led his Chichimecs into the central valley, where he built the core of what is now the wondrous seven–shelled pyramid of Tenayuca, a model for the later Aztec builders.

Of the divine twins, Xólotl has had a more curious and specific afterlife than Quetzalcóatl. The latter remained the Plumed Serpent, the former became a fat little hairless dog, the "*Xólotl-itzcuintli*" which guides men's souls into the realm of the dead as the evening star guides the dying sun. The *xóloizcuintle*, as he is now called, is the most amiable of creatures. We will run across him further on, in the pit–and–chamber burial vaults of *Occidente*, his polished red ceramic image still keeping the bones of his master company.

A novel architectural development of the Late Post–Classic was the carving of monuments in living rock. In Malinalco, the Aztecs achieved the most remarkable results in this technique of what is essentially monolithic sculpture. They carved a hillside of solid rock into a series of terraces, staircases, temples and even a round sanctuary, adorned with relief carvings of jaguars and eagles, emblems of the Aztecs' knightly military orders.

HIDALGO
(Named after Miguel Hidalgo y Costilla)

A mine, a convent, an hacienda. Based upon this trinity, the life of New Spain gradually took shape; the three coexisted all over New Spain, though the heartland states are possibly the region where they reached their most distinctive expression. In Hidalgo, the silver mine of Real del Monte, the Augustinian convent of Actopan, and the pulque hacienda of San Antonio Ometusco are the exemplars. Tula, the capital of the Toltecs, who prevailed in the Early Post–Classic (900–1200), is in the State of Hidalgo.

on an optimistic note. Mexico has in recent years developed into one of the richest states in the republic simply because of its proximity to Mexico City. The state surrounds the Federal District on three sides, enfolding also much of Morelos to the south, and therefore holds the country's richest market cupped within its boundaries.

The over–restored remains of Teotihuacán, the City of the Gods which dominated most of the Classic period in northern Mesoamerica, stand in what is now the state of Mexico. Tula, the capital of the Toltecs, who prevailed in the Early Post–Classic (900–1200), is in the state of Hidalgo.

In Teotihuacán, one should know that the Pyramid of the Moon antedates the Pyramid of the Sun. This suggests that the original Teotihuacanos may have been part of a matriarchal, moon–worshiping culture. If so, the building of the much larger Pyramid of the Sun would represent the displacement of the matriarchal by the patriarchal, sun–worshiping society. The later Aztec eagle–serpent pictograph for Tenochtitlán now Mexico's national emblem, may be its most definitive expression.

THE MINE: REAL DEL MONTE

Zacatecas, Hidalgo, and Guanajuato are the earliest significant mining centers established after the Conquest. The first silver strikes in Pachuca and nearby Real del Monte took place in 1552 and were so spectacular that the word *pachocha*, a corruption of Pachuca, became in popular speech a slang synonym for wealth. What is known as the patio system of silver extraction by means of amalgamation with quicksilver was invented in Pachuca in 1555 by the Spaniard Bartolomé de Medina. This gave silver mining great impetus, but also made New Spain more dependent than ever on Spain because of Spain's virtual monopoly on the production of quicksilver.

The first silver boom, which started with the Zacatecas strikes of 1548 followed by those of Guanajuato, Pachuca and Real del Monte in 1552, financed the exploration and settlement of the northern provinces, the development of Peru, and the conquest of the Philippines. The second boom, which began in Real del Monte about 1740, financed the second – and greater, if less permanent – northward expansion, which more than doubled the territory of New Spain.

The flooded Vizcaína mines in Real del Monte sparked the second boom when miners struck the mother lode using a new method of draining the mine, not from the top but the bottom by aiming and boring a tunnel from the foot of the mountain to the foot of the mine shaft and letting the water run out of its own accord.

Fanny Calderón, visiting Real del Monte in 1840, provides details of a more gossipy nature: "The whole country here, as well as the mines, formerly belonged to the Count of Regla, who was so wealthy that when his son, the father of the present Count, was christened, the whole party walked from his house to the church upon ingots of silver. The Countess, having quarreled with the Vicereyne, sent her in token of reconciliation a white satin slipper entirely covered with large diamonds. The Count invited the King of Spain to visit his Mexican territories, assuring him that the hoofs of His Majesty's horse should touch nothing but solid silver from Veracruz to the capital. This last would be accomplished by shoeing His Majesty's horse in silver, one presumes."

Mexico's struggle for independence had kept the country in turmoil between 1810 and 1821. The mines were abandoned and the mining industry subsided for the duration. Mexico's independence from Spain, however, suddenly made Mexican investments particularly attractive to other Europeans, especially the English. In 1824, Real del Monte stock was offered in London and suddenly a silver fever as acute as the tulip craze of the 1600's seized England. The Real del Monte bubble burst in 1848 after British investors lost over one million pounds.

Mexico's mineral wealth backfired from the beginning. The first boom produced such inflation in Spain that wages rose 300 percent between 1550 and 1620, which left Spain defenseless against the cheaper and more abundant goods of northern Europe. Spain tried to protect itself in the mercantilist fashion of the times by establishing a hermetic monopoly on trade with its New World colonies and, in addition, by outlawing all industrial competition from the colonies themselves. New Spain, hampered in every effort to develop industrially, was forced to buy its manufactured goods from Spain with bullion. It lived off capital from the beginning and never learned to create a competitive capital–goods industry. And so, finding a mine or its equivalent – a buried treasure – became from the earliest times the national dream, beyond which the average Mexican mentality has not progressed. A lottery-of-life psychology developed which has closed, bolted, and barred the door to anything like a national work ethic. The Virgin of Guadalupe or a lottery *cachito* (1/20 of a ticket) can make any one a millionaire overnight. In Mexico even the most successful buy reams of lottery tickets, which may be the peak of greediness, but is perhaps inevitable in a country whose prosperity has always depended on finding one more silver mine and ever more abundant oil fields.

The Convent: Actopan

If a traveler can visit only one colonial monument in Mexico, the knowledgeable agree that it should be the Augustinian convent of Actopan. It is a compendium of the architectural idioms in use in the middle of the sixteenth century.

Since the Franciscans had arrived first, the Augustinians were forced to venture further afield. They went north to the Gran Chichimeca and west to the Tarascan Kingdom of Michoacán. As labor was scarce there, the Augustinians built less and more slowly than either the Franciscans in central Mexico or the Dominicans in the south. The important buildings they did put up, however, remain monuments to their high ambition. They built like city planners rather than architects, and their convent in Yuriría, Michoacán, for example, achieved majestic proportions.

Actopan, like most sixteenth–century convents in New Spain, illustrates the transition from the Gothic style to the round arch of the Plateresque, as the Renaissance style is called in Spain and its colonies. The cloister, for instance, has groined vaults and tall Gothic arches on the ground floor, while the floor above has double round arches over every pointed arch below. Originally, the light Gothic skeleton evolved out of the sturdy Romanesque body to capture the hesitant light of northern Europe. Now in the New World it faced two contrary stimuli: the stylistic change to the neo-Romanesque of the Renaissance, and the hot summers and radiant skies, which would necessitate smaller windows and a heavier building fabric. Throughout the sixteenth century, Gothic ribbings continued to appear in church interiors,

though more for aesthetic than for structural reasons. In the end, however, the round arch prevailed, with its correspondingly massive walls. The climate has the final say in all good building. The first Viceroy, Antonio de Mendoza, keenly aware of the importance of convents, thought it convenient to establish a set of rules regarding their architectural organization. Among the things he decreed was that all convents should be built facing west. So one must stand with one's back to the afternoon sun in order to appreciate the originality of Actopan. Adjoining the church on its north side, and at the far end of the atrium, rises the huge arch of its open chapel, Mexico's unique contribution to ecclesiastical architecture. It was designed to accommodate the multitudes who thronged to Mass and could not be fitted inside the church. In the open chapel, Mass was said in the vernacular for their special benefit. The Actopan open chapel is a tour de force of engineering. Deceptively light in appearance, the span of its barrel vault measures 17.5 meters across, which makes it wider than the naves of Nôtre Dame in Paris, of Amiens, Toledo, or Seville. It is three meters wider than the nave of the Actopan church itself, and is made to look considerably bigger by its trompe l'oeil coffered ceiling. The cloister, aside from its Gothic-Renaissance hybrid character, has a further point of interest. The wide stairwell has walls covered on all four sides by perfectly-preserved black and white murals depicting genre scenes from the conventual life of the followers of Saint Augustine. These murals provide us with the fullest inventory of sixteenth-

century objects and furnishings. The refectory to the south of the cloister has a coffered barrel vault similar to the one in the open chapel, although not on such a vast scale. This is much longer, but lower and narrower. The trompe l'oeil effect of the coffering is here so perfect that it takes a minute to realize that it is real coffering recessed into the fabric of the vault and painted there to suggest a trompe l'oeil. The doors and windows offer another delicious surprise. Cut diagonally through the massive masonry to the walls on an axis that crosses a corner of the room and goes out through another similarly biased door, these openings catch every breeze but will not allow a direct view into the room. This is functionalism of the highest order.

Mexico. A typical, though particularly large, central patio in a hacienda, and opposite page: a detail from the same hacienda.

THE HACIENDA

Haciendas under other names – *fincas*, plantations, *cortijos* – exist throughout the world, but a *pulque* hacienda exists only in Mexico. And even in Mexico, only the central states produce *pulque*. This pre-Hispanic drink, fermented from the juice of the giant agave, enjoyed such extraordinary popularity that the Aztec lawgivers made pulque drinking a capital offense for all able-bodied men under the age of sixty. A first offender's hair was cropped; a second offender's house was razed to the ground; a man found drunk for the third time was sacrificed with his entire family. Yet pulque continued to be produced and secretly drunk. All sorts of myth and ritual surrounded the pulque. The celebrants of the pulque cult had to be over sixty, of course. Their deity was a rabbit ritually called *Ome Toachtli* ("Two-Rabbit") the god of drunkenness, making Ometusco, by its name alone, the archetype of all pulque haciendas.

The overgrazed soils of Apan, the wind-swept, hail-smitten plains of southern Hidalgo, are the favorite habitat of the *maguey*, as the pulque agave is known. The proximity of the Mexico City market, moreover, made the maguey the ideal crop for the local landowners. Between 1785 and 1789 it was the Crown's fourth most important source of revenue. In Don Porfirio's time, especially after the arrival of the Veracruz-to-Mexico railroad, pulque haciendas became gilt-edged investments for the landed gentry, producing a low but steady income which could not be matched by the wheat, corn, beans, or other crops which were vulnerable to pests, diseases, and the frequent hailstorms of the area. In this affluent period, the "pulque aristocracy" joined the oligarchy of the silver aristocracy and the cattle barons of the north.

The pommel of an 18th century sword.

The typical charro (sombrero) and sarape made of what Queen Elizabeth I called the finest cloth, a blend of wool and silk.

Opposite page: an 18th century sculpture of the Virgin in the hacienda chapel.

Guanajuato. Augustinian convent of Yuriria, 16th century.

Querétaro and Guanajuato

Querétaro and Guanajuato are known together, with a fine disregard for originality but a strict respect for truth, as "The Cradle of our Independence." Nothing else in the area, not the prodigious lodes of La Valenciana, nor the vast haciendas, the gilded altars of Querétaro, nor the spectacular flowering of the Baroque with its stone façades, can match the importance of the Insurgency sparked by Miguel Hidalgo, the priest from Dolores, Guanajuato, and the Creole conspirators in Querétaro.

An Indian pueblo conquered in 1532, Querétaro was the older city. It flourished as a presidio-garrison town and trading post on the Zacatecas silver route as early as 1550. The discovery of the Guanajuato mines between 1552 and 1556 created a brisk additional demand, and valley towns like San Miguel el Grande (now "Allende") and Celaya prospered along with Querétaro. During the heavy eighteenth-century influx of immigrants from northern Spain, the Querétaro-Guanajuato economy reached its colonial peak. Merchants, textile manufacturers, hacendados, and miners intermarried and invested in one another's ventures. Their *obrajes* (textile mills), their haciendas, their mines were the richest and best managed in Mexico. The merchants held the purse strings to all these ventures, gradually becoming investment bankers as well as traders. Members of the silver aristocracy went to the merchants for cash, discovered new lodes so that both parties became fabulously rich, like Obregón (a miner) and Otero (a merchant), whom the Valenciana mine made the richest men in the world.

Guanajuato. Church of the Valenciana.

Opposite page: ornate Churigueresque Baroque façade.

Above: same church seen from the city walls.

Right: the church's colorful setting.

167

THE CONSPIRACY OF MARTÍN CORTÉS (1565–1568)

Guanajuato. San Miguel de Allende. The peaceful cobblestone town comes to life through its colors. Collage of local façades.

A powerful society of self-made men invariably rebels against colonial status. The first, unsuccessful, example of this phenomenon occurred in New Spain shortly after the Conquest; its leaders were the sons of Cortés and his captains. It must be kept in mind that the Conquest, like other early ventures of that sort, was a result of private enterprise on the part of the conquistadors, so they looked on their *encomiendas* as the spoils of war. They had risked their lives and fortunes for them, while the Crown had risked nothing. The *encomenderos* could hardly know that the Crown saw their power in New Spain as a threat to its sovereignty. The New Laws of 1542 were the Crown's first step in the demolition of the nascent feudalism in New Spain. The Mendicant Friars cheered, but the encomenderos howled and decided to secede from Spain and to establish their own monarchy in the New World. They

chose as their leader Martín Cortés, the son of the Conquistador, newly arrived from the Spanish court and invested with the glamour of being Philip II's friend. Given a royal welcome by the Viceroy Luis de Velasco, Martín Cortés immediately antagonized him. The conspirators applauded and became rasher by the minute. They discussed their plot openly and swaggered before the Crown officials. Their insolence became a public scandal.

They did not have long to wait for an answer. Martín Cortés was easily flattered into the first trap laid for him. Arrested as he arrived at the Audiencia's offices in the viceregal palace, he was accused of treason and put in prison together with the principal conspirators. Some were summarily executed. Martín Cortés and his half-brothers were sent to Spain to stand trial. Though his estate, sequestered by the Crown in 1567, was returned in 1574, Martín never returned to New Spain.

The Mexican Enlightenment

This aborted conspiracy only confirmed the defeat inflicted by Charles V on the rebellious Spanish *comunidades* in 1521.The Crown became increasingly powerful. It created *corregimientos* – Crown encomiendas – to govern all free townships and cities while the private encomienda system was being dismantled. It also supported the secular clergy against the regular clergy, whose immense influence with the natives represented another threat to the power of the Crown. Peninsular clergy, considered more trustworthy than Creoles, Indians, or Mestizos, received most preferments, and the Jesuits, whose company was created to counteract the disintegrating effect of the Reformation, were sent to New Spain in 1572, where they established the most influential school system to date.

During their first 150 years in New Spain, the Jesuits became the mentors of the ruling class. They built great colleges and established missions in the most ungrateful outposts of the Sonora and California deserts. In the course of the eighteenth century, however, they did an intellectual about-face that would have pained their founder as much as it pained their monarch. A large number of Central European Jesuits had volunteered for missionary work in Mexico. They arrived trailing the heady ideas of the Enlightenment in their wake. They taught their students, the brilliant young Miguel Hidalgo among them, to read Rousseau and the Philosophes, and to think for themselves. Debating clubs sprang up under the guise of literary societies. Short-lived newspapers spread the infection that began to pose a serious threat to the authority of the monarchy. Charles III decided to act. Being an enlightened despot (that is, the only man in the realm who can hold enlightened views without being subversive) he decided to get rid of the Jesuits. In 1767 he expelled the Company of Jesus from

Guanajuato. San Miguel Allende. A roof garden with view on the Church of San Miguel.

Spain and its dominions by a ban reading: "Let it be known by the following that the subjects of His Majesty, King of Spain, were born to be silent and to obey in silence and not to discuss and express opinions on the high affairs of the government." Free thought, however, is more addictive than any alkaloid, and the Jesuits' influence was irreversible. The Jesuits had trained several generations to think for themselves, and they became an irresistible force in public opinion. Conspiracies proliferated in various provincial capitals, inspired first by the American and then by the French Revolution. The Rights of Man replaced the Apostles' Creed.

MIGUEL HIDALGO Y COSTILLA (1753–1811)

The power vacuum in Spain set the viceregal edifice trembling. Such unstable times seemed made to order for the parish priest of Dolores, Miguel Hidalgo y Costilla, one of the most independent and idiosyncratic men ever born.

Ordained at the age of twenty-five, he was assigned lucrative livings but generally left the running of the churches to his curates while devoting himself to scientific research and experimental farming. His outspokenness in local *tertulias*, his musical evenings with dancing, his tangled financial affairs, the birth of yet another child with yet another woman, kept him from advancement in the church. In 1802 his elder brother died, and Hidalgo succeeded to his parish in Dolores, where he continued his style of life to the delight of his new neighbors .

He made friends with Ignacio Allende, a captain in the royal army, who was a well-to-do Creole, son of Spanish parents, from San Miguel el Grande (now called San Miguel de Allende in his honor). They had similar political views. They agreed that Mexico should break away from the fraudulent monarchy of Pepe Botellas ("Joe Bottles," as Napoleon's bibulous brother on the Spanish throne was called). In Querétaro, the wife of the Corregidor subscribed to this view and her house became the center of a conspiracy. Similar revolutionary juntas had been established in San Miguel, Celaya,

Guanajuato, San Luis Potos' and Mexico City. December 1, 1810 was the date set for the *pronunciamiento*. Hidalgo, the brilliant ideologue and persuasive speaker, was chosen to head the movement. In a moment of tragic pride, he accepted. The Querétaro junta sprang a leak and soon the royalist police besieged the Corregidor's house. Hearing the news in Dolores, on the eve of 16 September, Hidalgo saw that the die was cast and uttered the famous *Grito de Dolores*, the rallying cry of the Insurgency.

Followed by armed civilians, he took a banner of the Virgin of Guadalupe and made it the flag of the movement. His campaign was brief: seven months of politics and fighting, followed by four months in prison, standing trial, and waiting for his death sentence to be carried out. He was executed in Chihuahua on 30 July 1811 and Mexico did not become independent until 1821.

THE SILVER CONQUEST OF THE NORTH: ZACATECAS, AGUASCALIENTES, DURANGO, SAN LUIS POTOS'

Each of these states grew around a city of the same name which is now its capital. They all owe their existence directly or indirectly to Zacatecas, for the silver strikes of 1548 that overnight turned Zacatecas into the second city of New Spain also made it the metropolis of the north. Made bold by the Zacatecas bonanza, the entire floating population of New Spain rushed toward the inhospitable mountains of the Gran Chichimeca. Some prospectors found silver closer to Mexico City, in places like Pachuca, Real del Monte, and Guanajuato. The traders and the farmers followed, creating new towns, among the most successful of which was Aguascalientes, which became a separate state in 1857, and continues to derive great prosperity from agriculture.

Two key figures stand out in the foundation of Zacatecas; Juan de Tolosa and Diego de Ibarra. Tolosa was married to the most aristocratic mestiza in New Spain, Doña Leonor Cortés Moctezuma, daughter of the conquistador and granddaughter of the Aztec Emperor. Like most of the conquistadors, he had heard about silver mines in the north.

Following a friendly and informative Indian guide, he was the first to find silver–bearing rocks in a wild spot below a hill with a sinister rocky excrescence on the top which he named *la Bufa* ("pig's bladder" in Basque). Only Diego de Ibarra believed in his discovery and followed him. Ibarra, like Tolosa, had high connections in New Spain. He married the daughter of the future Viceroy, Luis de Velasco, and placed his young nephew, Francisco de Ibarra, in the Viceroy's court. The Zacatecas silver strike showed the advisability of further exploration to the north. The Viceroy commissioned the young Ibarra boy to undertake the task. Francisco de Ibarra went to Zacatecas and, with his rich uncle's backing, organized an expeditionary force for the purpose and set off in 1554. He was sixteen years old at the time.

Endowed with the touch of a modest Midas, Francisco found silver wherever he went. In what is now the State of Durango, he founded the city which now bears that name as well as many other towns still in existence, though none of comparable importance.

San Luis Potos' remained throughout most of the sixteenth century a vast wilderness in the north–eastern portion of the Gran Chichimeca. It was the terrain of the indomitable Guachichiles, who held out against every assault for over forty years.

After the Zacatecas boom, however, the Spaniards were determined to conquer the land. That was the beginning of the Chichimec war, which lasted from 1552 to 1591. The Guachichiles' guerilla tactics, so swift and unexpected and, above all, so different from the ceremonial warring of the Aztecs, made them invulnerable to the Spanish soldiery. They struck suddenly, and as suddenly disappeared into the mountains, leaving trails in different directions. The Spanish forces could make no headway against them. The war did not end until military tactics were replaced by palavering

and gift offerings. The men chiefly responsible for this break were a Spanish–born Franciscan from Zacatecas, Fray Diego de la Magdalena, and a Mestizo captain, Miguel Caldera.

Fray Diego, a man who took both Christ and Saint Francis at their word, approached the Guachichil-Chichimecs with exemplary courage and sweetness. In 1583 he succeeded in persuading a group of them to cease their nomadic life and start learning the arts necessary for a settled existence. Four years later, Captain Caldera, comparing Fray Diego's success with the failure of armed conflict, prevailed upon the Viceroy, Luis de Velasco II, to support him in the innovative strategy of winning a war by peaceful means. Caldera was the son of a Spanish miner and a Guachichil woman, so he could talk to the Indians in their own language, and prove by his mere presence among them the possibility of peaceful co–existence with the Spaniards. Peace was finally achieved when Fray Diego and Captain Caldera convinced the Guachichiles that no tribute would be expected of them, only respect for the Spanish religious and civil foundations.

Shortly after peace was concluded, the first lodes were discovered and prospectors and traders swarmed to the new province. Though these states are relatively poor in pre–Hispanic remains, they are rich in Baroque splendors. The silver from the mines has paid for the gold of the altarpieces and the flowering stone of the doorways and façades. Still, if it is true that words outlast marble, gold, and bronze, then the poetry of a single Zacatecano, Ramón López Velarde (1888–1921), may well outlast all the palaces and churches of the region. His oeuvre is small, but one of his poems, *Suave Patria*, a celebration of Mexico's provincial life, has become the national epic. Yet its scale is intimate and its images belong to our common childhood. *Suave Patria* is a recreation of provincial Mexico in

Pancho Villa, one of the most picturesque revolutionary generals.

Zacatecas. Rear view of the Church of San Augustín.

Opposite page: Zacatecas. Principal portal of the Cathedral, the Churigueresque style here reaches its maximum expression.

the early years of this century, a scene observed through a child's eye and preserved in a child's memory. (Diego Rivera's mural of a childhood holiday in the Alameda, now in the lobby of the Prado Hotel across the street from the Alameda, could serve as an illustration for *Suave Patria*.) After school hours, the child buys sweets and toy balloons, drinks a glass of chía water, all the while thinking of this geography and history lessons, of Cortés and Cuauhtémoc and, reflecting on the Mexican sky, describes it as the smooth panning of herons and "the green lightening of the parrot's flight." He knows that the God-Child deeded us a stable and that our oil comes from the devil.

Cultura de Occidente: Michoacán, Colima, Jalisco, Nayarit Michoacán

(Náhuatl, *michihuacan*, "place of fishermen" from *michin*, fish, the possessive *hua* and the place ending can)

The pre-Hispanic Tarascos were probably the only Mesoamerican people who came up from the south. Their language, metallurgy, and hillside ter- race farming, as well as their pit-and-chamber burial vaults, clearly link them to some of the early cultures in Peru. Though repeatedly invaded by Teotihuácanos, Toltecs, and Aztecs, they managed to preserve their cultural and political autonomy.

Though their kingdom bears the Náhuatl name of Michoacán, all other place names surviving from pre-Hispanic times remained stubbornly *Purepecha*. (The Tarascos, incidentally, call themselves "*Purepechas*." Tarscue, i.e. Tarasco, is what they called the Spaniards. It means son-in-law in Purepecha, for they too had given their nubile daughters to the conquerors, and in the general linguistic muddle the Spaniards took it to mean the name of their race.)

Their cosmogony and religion had many similarities with those of the Aztecs, but again they managed to keep their own names for the deities and the concepts they borrowed from their powerful neighbors. One coincidence is that both Tarascos and Aztecs had a deity of filth and excrement, Xaranga and Tlazolteotl respectively, whose names exactly correspond to the Romans' Cloacina, deity of the sewers (*cloacas*).

Michoacan.
Centuries-old olive
trees in the
Franciscan Convent
of Tzintzuntzan.

Vasco de Quiroga (1470–1565)

The Mexican West was abysmally unlucky in its conquistadors, and correspondingly fortunate in its missionaries.

The Tarascos' behavior during the Conquest can hardly be faulted. They defended their neutrality with as much verve as their independence. Their King Zuanga, who had once repelled an attack by Moctezuma II, refused the Aztecs' help against the Spaniards. After Zuanga's death, twelve Aztec nobles approached his son, King Tangaxoan, with the same request. The Tarascos sacrificed them so that they could take their message personally to the dead king. Despite such adamantine attitudes, Cortés had no trouble in making friends with them. King Tangaxoan traveled to Coyoacán to meet Cortés and swear fealty to the Spanish emperor. Tangaxoan, baptized with the name of Don Pedro, in 1524 invited the Franciscans to send missionaries to Michoacán.

So matters stood when Nuño de Guzmán was called from the governorship of Pánuco to form part of the First Audiencia of New Spain (1527–30). Although traditionally credited with the conquest of the west and the creation of the Reign of New Galicia, what he actually did was slaughter the native population and leave a trail of bloodshed and terror wherever he went. Denounced before the Crown by Bishop Zumárraga, he left Mexico City, presumably to go in search of the City of the Amazons, of which he had heard exciting reports. Arriving in Michoacán, he demanded tribute from the converted king, Don Pedro de Tangaxoan. Dissatisfied with the amount, he hanged this friend of Cortés and vassal of Charles V. In Jalisco he burned over eight-hundred Indian pueblos and had their leaders *aperreados* (hounded), a process which consisted of chaining them together naked and having them torn apart by hunting dogs. He branded the natives he captured, and sold them to his followers at a peso a head.

The First Audiencia had been suspended and arraigned in his absence. Cortés returned from Madrid followed by the Second Audiencia in January 1531. A posse was sent to bring Nuño de Guzmán back to Mexico City to face charges, but by the time they found him, Guzmán had already received his royal appointment as Governor of New Galicia. He took the envoys prisoner, and from that time on made it a point to defy the Second Audiencia of New Spain. Finally, in 1536, he decided to present his case personally before the King. He had the misfortune to arrive in Mexico at the same time as the official who had been appointed to hear his case and replace him as governor of New Galicia. They met at the door of the Viceroy's apartments, and the new governor took Guzmán prisoner then and there. He was sent back to Spain, where he stood trial, received his sentence, and spent the rest of his life in jail.

The Second Audiencia had all the virtues that the first one lacked. With it came Vasco de Quiroga, perhaps the only man capable of counteracting the evil done by Nuño de Guzmán in the western territories. He spent 1533 and 1534 assessing the damage done in Michoacán. The enraged and now bitterly rebellious Tarascos would not come down from the hills to which they had fled after their experience with Guzmán. Seeing the hatred and mistrust Guzmán had planted in these steadfast spirits, Vasco de Quiroga understood that winning back their trust was destined to be his life's work.

The diocese of Michoacán was created in 1536 and Vasco de Quiroga was elected Bishop. But there was an obstacle: he was not even a priest. So in 1538 he was ordained and consecrated Bishop on the same day – perhaps a first and only case in modern ecclesiastical history. The cornerstone of his missionary work was to be the *"hospital-pueblo"*: the infirmary and hostelry for Indian pilgrims and travelers, the municipal offices, and the quarters for the groups of married volunteers who did the nursing and housekeeping. Quiroga decreed that every church should have a hospital and a school. At his death in 1565, he left ninety-two hospitals in his diocese.

After his death, the Jesuits took over his schools, including the one where young Miguel Hidalgo had picked up all his odd ideas, while the Augustinians elaborated on his primitive institutions by gathering whole native villages around their convents, which became teaching centers where new farming practices were tried out, European crops and fruit trees were planted, and where the natives could practice their traditional crafts and learn new ones. As a result of Vasco's and the friars' early teachings, Michoacán now has one of the richest and most varied traditions in handicrafts. Paracho continues to make guitars, Uruapán lacquer work, Pátzcuaro feather decorations, Santa Clara copper ware and Tzintzuntzán, a magical green-glaze ceramic that transcends rococo.

COLIMA
(Náhuatl, *Colliman*, "place of Colli," the aged hunchback god, bearer of fire, a reference to the nearby *Volcan del Fuego*)

Tenochtitlán conquered, Cortés sent his captains towards every point of the compass to explore and take possession of the land. The west fell to the lot of Cristóbal de Olid, whose peaceful takeover of the Tarascan kingdom in 1522 was so successful. King Colliman, on the other hand, proved unexpectedly tough. It took a second expedition, strengthened by several thousand Tarascos, to defeat him and to found, in 1523, the village of Colima, the first municipality in New Spain. Finding the climate unbearable, the leader of the expedition returned to Mexico City. Colima was a hardship post no one wanted.

It was in danger of reverting to nature, or to the natives, when Cortés remembered a young relation of his, Francisco Cortés de Buenaventura, and offered him the post, adding as an inducement the story of the City of the Amazons – "where no men ever were" – and a commission to seek it out and conquer it. Young Cortés could not contain his enthusiasm and soon set out on a new expedition. The youthful troops followed the captain, hacking their way enthusiastically through the underbrush, walking streams and skirting swamps, sustained by their romantic vision. They went as far north as Tepic before discouragement set in. The closest they came to finding a city of Amazons was in the nearby town of Xalixco, which was ruled by a woman.

On their return journey, young Cortés and his men were met by apparitions. In a valley near a beautiful bay, the dense underbrush suddenly blossomed into a myriad of colored flags, and Indians jumped out, disposed to fight. Though startled at first, the Spaniards shot a volley into the tree-tops. The natives at once proved amendable to reason, and a truce was reached. The spot is still called the Valley of Flags (Valle de Bandaras) in memory of the occasion, and owes its name to the nearby Bahía de Banderas, site of the lyrically lovely ex-village of Puerto Vallarta.

The Spaniards moved the original town of Colima from the torrid lowlands to the pleasant valley under the volcano where it now stands. This snow-capped cone rising above the mango and coconut groves of Colima dominates everything around it, the feathery, dark ravines, the intensely cultivated fields, even the glint of the faraway sea and the daily extravaganza put on by the setting sun.

NAYARIT
Name of the founder of the kingdom of the Cora Indians

New Galicia was Nuño de Guzmán's brainchild, the offspring of his megalomania and his gnawing envy of Cortés. At its height it comprised part of Zacatecas, Aguascalientes, San Luis Potosí, Durango, and Sinaloa, and all of Jalisco and Nayarit. In 1532, after receiving the charter of New Galicia and his appointment as governor, Nuño founded his capital in Tepic, which he called Compostela. After his death, one of his successors moved Compostela to a valley south of Tepic in 1540. The following year the Indians rose up in arms against the Spaniards throughout New Galicia, from the northernmost settlement of

Culiacán, in Sinaloa, to Guadalajara. Such Indian revolts led to the creation of the *Audiencia* of New Galicia in 1548, subject to the Audiencia of New Spain in Mexico City. The members of this Audiencia were a vicious lot. Though they had neither the power nor the autonomy enjoyed by Nuño de Guzmán and the First Audiencia of New Spain, they were far enough from Mexico City to do a great deal of damage before they were suspended and arraigned in 1558. The capital of New Galicia, the Audiencia, and the diocese, were then moved from Compostela to Guadalajara in 1560, a date which marks the effective beginning of Guadalajara's subsequent power, and Jalisco's overwhelming importance in western Mexico.

JALISCO

(Náhuatl, *xalixco*, "on a sandy plain," from *xalli*, sand, *ixtli*, surface, and locative ending – *co*).
Capital: Guadalaijara (Aarabic, *wadi-al-hajara*, "river of pebbles.")

Guadalajara, despite its early foundation in 1532, had inauspicious and precarious beginnings. It was founded first here, then moved there, then somewhere else, like a chess piece in Guzmán's New Galicia power game against New Spain, until it finally settled down in 1540 and grew roots in its present site. It was still a very small town in 1700, with a population of roughly 500 Creoles, 500 Negro and Mulatto slaves, and 500 Mestizos. By that time, however, the surrounding mines had been pouring their bullion into Guadalajara's coffers for a long time, and the wealth was beginning to show in the solid government buildings and the convents scattered about – all built in the golden quarry stone that gives Guadalajara's architecture its distinctive late afternoon glow.

San Blas had converted Guadalajara from a modest provincial capital at the start of the Insurgency in 1810 into the second city of the new republic. After the transfer of the Audiencia and See from Compostela to Guadalajara, probably no event had a greater influence on this city than the construction of the port at San Blas.

As early as 1767, that corporate trouble-shooter and efficiency expert of the Bourbon kings of Spain, José de Gálvez, had decided two things: that New Spain should be divided into *Intendancies*, and that a northern naval base and shipyards were indispensable and should be established in the bay of San Blas. The port was eventually built, and in 1768 the first small fleet sailed out of San Blas toward the Californias, carrying a detachment of troops and some Jesuit missionaries. In 1788 two frigates sailed north and did not turn back until they had established contact with the Russian fur traders in Alaska. But it was the Mexican War of Independence that lifted San Blas into sudden prominence, and Guadalajara to wealth and power.

The first wave of the Insurgency fizzled out in New Galicia. The Nayarit insurgents were routed, and the royalist troops cleared the road between Guadalajara and San Blas. As the war cut New Galicia off from its markets and suppliers – central Mexico was a battlefield and Veracruz lived under permanent siege – San Blas became the port of entry for all foreign goods, and Guadalajara became the distribution center for northwestern Mexico.

The trade route that developed between San Blas and Guadalajara laid the foundations for the latter's prosperity. Guadalajara teemed with new arrivals form every walk of life. Peasants and hacendados flocked to the city for safety, taking their valuables with them. Tradesmen and professional men found a brisk demand for their talents. In the first few years of the war, the population increased from thirty – to forty thousand. This sudden affluence showed in the face of the city. A building boom followed after the war, gathering in a sumptuous architectural effect the widely scattered monuments of its Baroque and neoclassical past. Garden squares framed churches, and blocks of arcades framed the squares. And throughout the city, the same golden quarry stone that built the earliest convents and palaces continued to provide the basso continuo for the noble urban harmonies of Guadalajara.

Jalisco. Costa Careyes. View over the Atlantic with an organ cactus in the foreground.
Below: A typical terrace of painted terracotta and tiles.

Jalisco. Steam rises from the lake at the bottom of a canyon near a volcano.

Opposite page: Jalisco. View of the Volcano Nevada de Colima.

CHAPTER 5

The Frontier States

Chihuahua. Shepherdesses of the Tarahumara tribe of Indians.

The States of Baja California and Baja California Sur, Coahuila, Chihuahua, Nuevo León, Tamaulipas, Sonora, Sinaloa

"The Loyalty March" mural by Juan O'Gorman, 1968. Chapultepec Castle.

The biggest and richest of Mexico's border states is Texas. The next biggest and richest is California. Unfortunately for Mexico, they are both now, and have been for over a hundred years, on the American side of the border. The time element is unimportant, though, and many Mexicans continue to experience flashing pains as a result of the amputation.

Spain had won and settled that land, Mexico had given it independence and freed the soil from slavery. Yet Mexico must take its share of blame for the loss if the enormity of the subsequent American injustice is to be seen in fair perspective. The now Republic of Mexico came out of its War of Independence totally depleted and lacking both

the human and the economic resources to maintain its enormous and empty northern territories. But instead of retrenching and reorganizing, it annexed an additional 180,000 square miles of the Central American provinces. Such over-extension made the new republic vulnerable on every side.

The first northern exploration with the arrival of the conquistadors was motivated by legends of the Golden Cities of Cibola, or Quivira. Hearsay reports of the golden cities led to the expedition of Francisco Vázquez de Coronado, who followed up the rumors and found nothing but straggles of adobe huts and the cliff side dwellings of the Pueblo Indians. His expedition made important discoveries, however, among them the Grand Canyon.

Beginning in 1581, expeditions explored the area that cartographers began to designate as New Mexico. In 1605 Santa Fé was founded, the second oldest city in the United States after Saint Augustine in Florida. Eighty years later the Governor of Nuevo Reino de León issued orders from Monterrey for the exploration and settlement of Texas with people from Saltillo, San Estéban de la Nueva Tlaxcala, and Monclova in the neighboring province of Coahuila. The colonization of Texas was carried out in the Roman style of civic and military outposts – in this case missions and *presidios* – rather than in the Anglo-Saxon fashion of homesteaders devoted to cultivating the land. Six missions were founded in 1716 and 1717, and San Antonio and El Alamo in the following year. Many were destroyed in the ensuing conflict. The Texas territory was established in 1727, though only its eastern border with Louisiana was defined.

The Louisiana Purchase of 1803 brought in an aggressive, expansionist American population. Three abortive American invasions were repelled until the Onís–Adams (Florida) Treaty between the United States and Spain defined the boundary lines. And the U.S. relinquished all claims on Texas. But in 1821 the newly–independent Mexico granted the American Moses Austin license to establish a foreign colony in Texas. Many southerners arrived with their slaves, in violation of Mexican law. Five years later the American Minister to Mexico, Joel Pointsett, offered to buy the eastern half of Texas for one million dollars but Mexico refused.

By 1830 Mexico woke up to the danger of unchecked immigration and closed the border, but there were already four Americans to every Mexican in Texas. Soon American settlers in San Antonio rejected the authority of the Coahuila-Texas government, and a secessionist movement began building among the Texas Americans. The secessionists set up a provisional government to fight for their independence. Sam Houston began hostilities against the virtually defenseless presidios which Mexico had long neglected. The patent weakness of the Mexican liberal–federalist party convinced even the anti-secessionists of the need to become independent. American homesteaders in Texas sought U.S. support.

From 6 March to 21 April 1836, Santa Anna besieged and massacred the men entrenched in the Alamo. Yelling "Remember the Alamo," Sam Houston defeated Santa Anna in San Jacinto, took him prisoner, and brought the war to an end. The Lone Star Republic was recognized by the U.S., Great Britain and France the following year.

Up to this point, Mexico must bear the blame for losing Texas. What happened next, though, will remain forever a blot on the history of the United States. California had been attracting more and more American immigrants and an important political group in Washington set its sights on the acquisition of California.

When The Lone Star Republic was admitted to the Union in 1845, Mexico broke diplomatic relations with the U.S. over the annexation of the rebellious province. In June of that year the U.S. Secretary of the Navy ordered Commodore Sloat to seize San Francisco as soon as war with Mexico was declared. In preparation for this eventuality, President James Polk sent an army detachment under General Zachary Taylor to the Nueces River, the southernmost boundary of Texas since its creation as a province of New Spain. Then Polk sent Minister Plenipotentiary John Slidell to Mexico with a set of proposals, including the extension of Texas south to the Rio Grande, the purchase of New Mexico which then included Arizona for five million dollars, and a "money-is-no-object" proposal for the purchase of California. Mexico did not receive Slidell.

Polk ordered General Taylor to cross the Nueces River and occupy the northern bank of the Rio Grande. Three months later the Mexican cavalry crossed the Rio Grande, killing some American soldiers and capturing the rest in the skirmish that followed. President Polk urged Congress to declare war against Mexico in the following terms:

"The cup of forbearance has been exhausted. After reiterated menaces, Mexico has passed the boundary of the United States, has invaded our territory and shed American blood upon American soil." On 13 May Congress declared war.

Polk did not go unchecked, however. A freshman Whig representative from Illinois by the name of Abraham Lincoln demanded that Polk reveal the exact spot on American soil where American blood had been shed. Receiving no answer from Polk, Lincoln again took the floor, accused Polk of provoking the war, and characterized his efforts to put the blame on Mexico as "the half-insane mumbles of a fever-dream." "The record is clear," wrote Morrison, Commager, and Leuchenburg in *A Concise History of the American Republic*." Polk baited Mexico into war over the Texas boundary in order to get California."

THE REVOLUTION

The Mexican north is still in many ways a bronco territory. It lacks the cultural unity that a dense population and a rich colonial culture gave the rest of the country as far north as the Zacatecas silver routes. The conquest and settlement of the northern states constituted the last, painfully prolonged stage of the Chichimec War. The Sonora Yaqui War, for example, only came to an end in 1937 with the signing of a treaty with President Cárdenas.

In this context, it is difficult not to see the 1910 Revolution as a sociological sequel to the ethnic conflicts of the many Chichimeca wars. The firmly-established south has always been the seat of government, imposing its will on the refractory north. Don Porfirio's regime was quintessentially southern in both geographical makeup and psychological outlook. Its overthrow represented an uprising of the north against the authority of the south. With the exception of Zapata, the leaders of the Revolution were all northerners.

Francisco I Madero was the scion of a rich Coahuila land-owning family. Though he held the economic views of his class, he rebelled against the political stranglehold of the southern hierarchy and Don Porfirio's dictatorship. To his own father's amazement, this singularly gentle son succeeded in carrying out the first legitimate election in thirty years and then ousting the dictator with a minimum of bloodshed. This he accomplished in exactly six months, from 20 November 1910, when the first shots were fired in Puebla, to 25 May 1911, when Don Porfirio signed his resignation in Ciudad Juárez, Chihuahua. With the dictator's removal the purpose of the Revolution was presumably accomplished. Very little Mexican blood had been shed. As it turned out, however, the Revolution had only just started, and it proceeded apace.

The maverick Pancho Villa dominated the phase of the Revolution beginning with Madero's uprising and ending with the 1917 Constitution. Born in Durango, he became an outlaw as a youngster after shooting his *hacendado* boss, whom he found trying to rape his sister. The Revolution was made to order for him. He had already moved on to Chihuahua by that time, and there he mounted the first rebel attacks on Ciudad Juárez and other border towns. Supported by his crack cavalry *División del Norte*, he became governor of Chihuahua from 1913 to 1915 (a fact most Mexicans ignore). In 1914 he broke with Carranza, the Constitutionalist leader, joined forces with Zapata, and went on with him to Mexico City.

After Pancho Villa's break with Carranza, "the strongmen of Sonora" came to the fore: Alvaro Obregón, the great warrior, and Plutarco Elias Calles, the consummate politician. Pancho Villa's apotheosis was the taking of Mexico City with Zapata and his men. After that, Villa's luck changed, or perhaps his marathon philandering took its toll. (He had in his personal guard a court entertainer who played the piano for him in his favorite brothels and restaurants, a fifteen-year-old lieutenant, Agustín Lara, who later became Mexico's most popular songwriter.) He lost battle after battle to Obregón in the central states; his Divisíon del Norte started melting away.

After that, he returned to his outlaw existence as a guerilla fighter in the Chihuahua mountains he knew so well. He returned to civil life after a general amnesty had been declared in 1920, someone must have found his presence too much of a potential threat. In 1923 Pancho Villa was ambushed and shot as he was driving back to his hacienda from a night in the town in Parral.

The sequel to Pancho Villa's story is singularly gruesome. In 1926, three years after his death, his grave was broken open and his corpse decapitated. But like Saint Anthony of Padua in life, Pancho Villa seems to have possessed the gift of ubiquity after death. For several years after the incident, traveling "carnivals" still showed the 5,000 dollars WANTED posters of Pancho Villa along with the "authentic head of the notorious Mexican bandit," many of which were exhibited simultaneously in different towns.

The period between the Aguascalientes Convention of 1914 and the shooting of President Carranza in 1920 was perhaps the bloodiest part of the Revolution. It took the next two presidents, Obregón (1920–24) and Calles (1924–28), all their time to rein in the wildly charging forces of a nation run amok. One rebellion succeeded another, all of which were successfully quelled. The most important was the Cristero Rebellion of 1926 to 1929, which ended when the government declared a general amnesty to the rebellious priests, though without changing one iota the "anti-clerical" constitutional articles that had provoked the outbreak.

In 1929, Calles, no longer president but definitely the strongman of Mexico, brought this wide-spread rebelliousness to an end with a stroke of political genius: the bringing together of all two hundred warring parties under one ecumenical umbrella, the PNR (Partido Nacional Revolucionario), grandfather of the present-day PRI (Partido Revolucionario Institucional), which was grandly designed to be all things to all men.

Ironically, this immensely effective institution created by a northerner became the political booty of the south practically from its inception. No northerner has since been elected president, although a couple of them have occupied the presidency in an interim status. This may seem an essentially frivolous observation until one looks back on Mexico's history. The north carried out the Revolution and left its progressive imprint on the 1917 Constitution. The party the northerners created to represent the will and the regional interests of the entire republic has been co-opted by southerners, who have formed a hereditary, oligarchic elite with a monopoly on political power that differs very little from the oligarchy expelled by the Revolution – except in the magnitude of the fortunes now amassed and in the extent of official corruption.

El Nuevo Reino de León

The settlement of the northern provinces of Nuevo León, Coahuila, and Tamaulipas, the "Second Conquest of New Spain," was carried out by later generations of conquistadors beginning in the second half of the sixteenth century and ending in the course of the eighteenth century with the settlement of Texas and the Californias and the conquest of Tamaulipas. Its history hinges on the fortunes of single cities, rather than of provinces, and as such it must be told.

The city of Saltillo had a precarious existence until 1589, when Miguel Caldera, the remarkable Mestizo captain who put an end to the Gran Chichimec war in San Luis Potosí two years later, arrived to palaver with the local Indians. Half-Guachichil himself, he convinced the Coahuila Chichimecs of the possibility of peaceful co-existence. The Viceroy Luis de Velasco II prevailed on the chief of the Tlaxcalan Republic to allow four hundred families to settle as homesteaders in the northern marches. In 1591 the rich Spanish miner Francisco de Urdinola, founded alongside Saltillo its Indian twin city of San Estéban de Nueva Tlaxcala.

Divided by the breadth of a single street, Saltillo and San Esteban were wolds apart in their judicial, religious and administrative organization. Saltillo depended judicially from the Audiencia of Guadalajara, administratively from Durango, capital of New Vizcaya, and ecclesiastically from the See of New Galicia, whereas San Estaban depended directly from the viceroy and the authority of the capital of New Spain. The Tlaxcalan settlers enjoyed privileges no other Indians had at the time. They could ride horseback, bear arms, place the honorific "don" (from *dominus*) before their names; best of all, they did not pay taxes either to the Guadalajara Audiencia or the New Vizcaya treasury. This most enviable of exemptions eventually erased the borderline between the two cities. San Esteban became a tax shelter for the Saltillo Spaniards and soon the distinction between the two cities disappeared. No discord developed between the two racial groups because their very distinct economic activities never came into competition. The Spaniards grew wheat, bred livestock and founded related industries such as flour mills, tanneries and textile mills, while the Tlazcalans grew vegetables, fruit trees and practiced their native handicrafts. Theirs were two complementary economies that enriched and never embittered their relationship.

Saltillo's prosperity and growth were such that it soon began to provide settlers for the less fortunate neighboring towns. Monterrey was one of its first beneficiaries. An exotic strain marks the town's beginnings. In 1579 Luis de la Cueva y Carvajal, a Portuguese of Jewish ancestry, received a charter from Philip II to explore, conquer, pacify, and settle a gigantic area that included most of what are now the states of Texas, Coahuila, Nuevo León and Tamaulipas. Carvajal brought with him many New Christians (converts from Judaism) exempted from providing proof of their religious orthodoxy and the purity of their blood, a remarkable concession on Philip II's part.

In 1579 Carvajal founded San Luis Rey de Francia on the site of the future Monterrey. The following year he went on to Saltillo, showed the inhabitants his charter, and recruited a sufficient number to found Almaden on the ruins of La Trinidad, whence he left to continue exploring the boundless lands of his charter. The lieutenant he left in Almaden, disappointed with the poverty of the mines, persuaded the remaining settlers to follow him north to what they began then to call New Mexico. None of their settlements survived.

The machinations of his enemies finally brought Carvajal to the tribunals of the Inquisition, accused of slave trading and being faithful to his old religion. He was arrested and taken to Mexico City; his wife and sister were also arrested, tortured, and burned at the stake. He died in the dungeons of the Inquisition in 1590 of what sounds suspiciously like a broken heart.

Shortly after Carvajal's arrest, his settlement was abandoned and the Indians burned it to the ground. In 1596 the treasurer of the town, Diego de Montemayor, decided to reconstruct the settlement, calling it Monterrey in honor of the reigning viceroy. Though the town did not founder again, it did not begin to grow and prosper until 1611, when a Zacatecas silver millionaire, Augustín de Zavala, was named governor of the province. Augustín de Zavala never showed up in Monterrey. He governed through agents and justices until his son Martín acquired a royal charter in Madrid and returned in 1626 to take over the management of the Nuevo Reino de León. He offered extensive grants for the settlement of Querétaro and San Miguel and shortly thereafter the first flocks of sheep arrived.

Sheep-raising turned out to be such a lucrative business that it soon became one of the preferred investments of the colonial nobility of New Spain. By the middle of the eighteenth century, flocks numbering millions migrated from Querétaro and Guanajuato to Nuevo León and Nuevo Santander (Tamaulipas), where they spent the winter, were sheared in the spring, and were herded back to their home pastures for the summer. This migratory type of sheep walk, though immensely profitable to the owners of the flocks, virtually destroyed the Nuevo León countryside, leaving it an overgrazed desert. The walks, however, blazed the trails for the missions, presidios, and entrepôts. The merchants who followed these trails naturally specialized in goods like corn fodder, hides, wool and its products, and in time established tanneries and woolen mills which were the first industries that appeared in Monterrey.

Coahuila remained a part of the Nuevo Reino de León until 1689, when Alonso de León, returning from his Texas expedition, ordered the resettlement of Almaden, which had become a ghost town, and called the new city Santiago de Monclova, upon which Coahuila became a separate province with Monclova as its capital.

Monclova, on the site of the pre–Hispanic Cuauhuilan, remained the capital of the province until 1824, when the first federal constitution of the Mexican republic made Saltillo the capital of Coahuila–Texas.

TAMAULIPAS

Nuevo León, Coahuila, and Texas moved into the eighteenth century under the aegis of Monterrey, which during the previous century had out–stripped every other northern city. Of all the provinces included in Carvajal's royal charter, only Tamaulipas stagnated. It was then still known as the Province of Pánuco, after the city founded by Cortés in 1522 on the Pánuco River, Tamaulipas's southern boundary. Many later missions and set–tlements failed. Pánuco itself barely survived. The plaguey swamps, the heat, the insects, the epi–demics drove all the would–be settlers out.

During his tenure of office in Pánuco, the unspeakable Nuño de Guzmán, true to type, did as much harm as anybody could in such a short time. The *encomiendas*, which had theoretically dis–appeared from New Spain by the 1650's, surfaced in Tamaulipas under the name of *congregas*, con–gregations of Indians held under exactly the same conditions as the early encomiendas. The con–gregas became slave markets and clearing centers.

The missionaries denounced the situation repeat–edly, with little effect. No new conquistadors could be persuaded to risk their capital in an unhealthy climate where no worthwhile mines had ever been found. The necessary stimulus finally came from the outside in the guise of the French sorties from the Louisiana territory into Texas. At the same time, English vessels made tentative land–ings along the Gulf coast. Such obvious threats moved the government of New Spain to take action. The coast between Pánuco and Corpus Christi was an open invitation to privateers. It had to be fortified and colonized at once.

When the bidding opened for the coloniza–tion charter, an army captain by the name of José de Escandón won hands down. Settled in Querétaro, he had foreseen the peremptory need to colonize Tamaulipas. Having wide experience and a methodical mind, he proceeded to explore the country at his own expense. In 1748 he received the charter to establish the province of New Santander in the lands of Tamaulipas. Escandón established experimental farms and irrigation systems around his presidio–villages. The network of roads and bridges he developed between the twenty–two permanent settlements he left at his death served as the base for the network of modern communications. The north–east conformed to the general pattern of Mexico's nineteenth–century history as outlined earlier in this book. The unremitting Indian wars frequently reached genocidal dimensions. The centrifugal force generated by the struggle between the cen–tralists and the federalists permanently lost us Texas, New Mexico, and Upper California, and almost lost us the Yucatán peninsula as well.

The economic development of the northern cities traces the country's general development far better than the minutely–detailed accounts of military movements and political intrigues that all too often pass for history. A glance at Torréon (Coahuila), Tampico (Tamaulipas), and Monterrey during the century and a half following Independence should suffice to make our point.

Chihuahua.
Tarahumara,
Romiguérachi.

Opposite page: The
Tarahumara tribe
were characterized
by their strength
and resistance and
their height being
superior to the
Indians in central
and southern
Mexico.

The Matachínes
are ritual dancers.
They dress up in
traditional costumes
and visit as many
towns and cities as
they can, where they
perform in the
atriums of churches.

TORRÉON

In 1825 the London banking firm of Baring Brothers bought the assets of the then bankrupt Marquesado de San Miguel de Aguayo in northern Mexico. The assets consisted mainly of vast tracts of land and sheep haciendas in the state of Coahuila. They included on their western boundary lines, adjoining Durango, the fertile land of the Nazas river valley, an area called La Laguna, where the city of Torréon would suddenly and surprisingly sprout a few decades later.

Baring Brothers found its Mexican venture ultimately unrewarding and gave up too soon, thereby losing properties that were soon to become among the most prosperous enterprises ever to flourish on Mexican soil. In 1840 Baring Brothers sold out to the Sánchez Navarro brothers, Jacobo and Carlos, two energetic *hacendados* whose family had accumulated a sizable *latifundio* in the course of the previous century. With the acquisition of the Marquesado lands, their consolidated haciendas constituted the largest privately-held estate in the entire American continent. On the map they covered a large part of the state of Coahuila, half the size of Belgium. Sánchez Navarro latifundio is, by its very size, the exemplar of the extensive cattle operation typical of the northern hacienda, as opposed to the smaller, though still very large southern haciendas devoted to intensive agriculture.

A farmer who bought the southwest corner of that vast estate immediately started an ambitious irrigation project of the Nazas River, which ran through the property, and Torréon takes its name from a tower at one end of the project's ramparts. Torréon was little more than a name until the building of the railroad from Mexico City to

*Non est dilata
fallacia, sed ad latus
navigii furtim
processimus
capitaque cum
supercilis
denudanda tonsori*

193

Ciudad Juárez and El Paso. A far-sighted real-estate man had subdivided all the land around the future railroad station and the railroad's arrival in 1888 turned his subdivision into the future city of Torréon. In 1902, the Coahuila-Pacific line joined Torréon to Saltillo, and it became the third most important railroad town in Mexico. Its inhabitants, a thrifty and creative race of farmers and merchants, have since made Torréon the crucial distribution center of northwestern Mexico.

Tampico

Boom towns and ghost towns attend every mineral bonanza, whether the result of silver, gold, uranium or oil strikes. Tampico, now a fairly prosperous port on the Gulf of Mexico, encloses in its economic fabric the ghost of a boom town whose per capita wealth was the highest in Mexico during the years of the Revolution and the First World War. Founded in 1828, Tampico made little mark on the regional economy until 1898, when the Pierce Oil Company built a refinery there for imported crude oils. The discovery of the *Faja de Oro* (Golden Strip) oil-fields, in northern Veracruz, combined with the onset of the First World War, made Tampico, with its refining and port capacity, briefly the oil shipping capital of the world. The town boomed right through the Mexican Revolution and the European war, despite the 1914 landing of the American Marines. While the rest of the country sank into a bog of unproductiveness and every local *caudillo* printed his own money (*bilimiques*), in Tampico, gold and silver coins were the common currency.

The seepage of salt water into the Faja de Oro oil wells brought Tampico's boom to an end in the early twenties. It had lasted long enough to leave a valuable and workable infrastructure of roads and port facilities which fostered the development of the hinterland and provided a ready market for its crops and livestock. The point of Tampico's story is simply that mineral wealth brings only transitory plenty, whereas lasting prosperity depends on an entirely different kind of economic activity – that of creating new wealth rather than simply extracting buried treasure from the earth. Tampico's prosperity outlived its boom years because a sufficient proportion of that treasure was transformed into productive capital.

Monterrey

Nature was not kind to Monterrey. Or rather, it was not generous, which, in the final tally, amounted to being most kind.

The valley's magnificence could not disguise the fact that the countryside was practically a desert, with bitter winters and summers like a furnace. Its richest mine, La Iguana, raised brief hopes in the 1750's, then petered out in less than ten years. Their hostile environment forced the *reineros* to adapt themselves to adversity by developing the puritanical work ethic that paid off so richly in the end. They put their capital to work when all the treasure of Mexico's mines had already been spent on inglorious and useless wars or on glorious and still useful buildings.

The American Civil War brought Monterrey its first substantial influx of capital. The Union blockade of Confederate ports obliged the southern cotton growers to ship their crops overland to Monterrey and thence to England via Matamoros. Many of Monterrey's founding fortunes had their origin in this windfall.

The defeat of the Confederacy brought Monterrey's prosperity to an end as sudden as its beginning. The railroads, which had made Torréon rich, deprived Monterrey of its importance as a commercial entrepôt. Merchants now bought directly from the producers and manufacturers. The nature of that depression showed the Monterrey capitalists the way out: they became producers and manufacturers themselves. They had made easy money as middlemen during the Civil War, but they saw that industrial production – especially the production of capital rather than consumer goods – would bring them a more lasting prosperity. Thus Monterrey became the industrial capital of the country around the turn of the century.

The inhabitants of Monterrey did not amass wealth for its own sake, the earmark of avarice, but put it to use in the creation of new industries. This, and other old-fashioned virtues, have given the citizenry of Monterrey an authority that has challenged and withstood the impositions of Mexico's most insolent and domineering regimes. Monterrey has now slipped from its premier industrial position in the country for political and demographic, rather than technical, reasons.

The States of Baja California and Baja California Sur, Chihuahua, Sonora, Sinaloa

Sinaloa and Baja California Sur are not border states, but they are most definitely frontier states and have been so since long before the arrival of the Spaniards. The frontier does not necessarily coincide with the border between the two countries. Its character is psychological rather than geographical. It represents the always-precarious equilibrium between the impulse to expand and the incapacity to do so.

We have already seen how the U.S.-Mexico border reached its present physical conformation. The frontier is something else, and both Sinaloa and Baja California Sur are good examples of non-border frontiers. Culiacán (the capital of Sinaloa), for instance, was for a long time the northernmost frontier of Mesoamerica, placed at the tip of a cultural peninsula that extended northward into the stormy lands of the nomadic Chichimecs. Culiacán was an independent seigneury at the time of the Conquest.

The Spanish town of Culiacán was founded in 1531 by Nuño de Guzmán. For a long time after its founding the Spanish city remained as isolated as the Mesoamerican town had been, and was in every sense the northernmost frontier of New Spain. In fact, after Guzmán's imprisonment, the Spanish authorities seemed to have forgotten about it. Even Francisco de Ibarra, the most illustrious of the second wave of conquistadors, had no idea that it existed. When he marched out of

Zacatecas, a precocious sixteen-year-old heading an almost equally youthful army, he skirted the Sierra Madre in a northwesterly direction, discovering silver mines and founding cities as he went. From Durango, his explorations branched north to Chihuahua and west toward Sinaloa.

One of his men registered the first of the silver mines in southern Chihuahua.

Unimportant as they seemed in comparison with the great *reales* of central Mexico, these mines tapped the northern tip of the geological strata known as the Zacatecas silver belt, and led to other discoveries which have made present-day Chihuahua Mexico's principal silver-producing state.

Even then, however, the new discoveries attracted the population necessary to keep the Indians at bay and start the haciendas needed to supply the mines with food and livestock. Cattle thrived in those virgin prairies and eventually the cattle barons became as rich as the miners and politically far more important. The mine-convent-hacienda formula that describes Mexico's heartland breaks down in the immensity of Chihuahua and the rest of the northern frontier states. The States are too big, and the mines too few and far between. This area developed along the line of the cattle ranch-mission-presidio colonization, which left great empty spaces open to foreign invasions.

When Ibarra descended from the high sierra to the torrid plains on the Pacific coast, instead of finding the wilderness and the savage Indians he expected, he came across the Spanish *encomendero* town of Culiacán, whose existence he had not been aware of. One of the more prosperous encomenderos talked him into marching north against the Yaquis of Sonora, who in 1533 had trounced the first Spanish expeditionary force.

Undaunted by the stories of the Yaquis' prowess as warriors, he proceeded to the heart of their country, a region then known as Ostímuri, between the Yaqui and the Mayo rivers. There he astonished his companions by approaching the

Next page: Chihuahua. Paquime culture. Ruins of Casas Grandes.

195

Culiacán remained the northern frontier post until the arrival of the Jesuits in 1591. Finding most of New Spain and its various sub-kingdoms pre-empted by the mendicant orders, the Jesuits directed their missionary efforts toward the north-western frontier. The nomadic Indians of the north only knew the Spaniards as warriors, predators, and despoilers of their land. Their hatred for the newcomers was richly deserved. The missionaries thus had to spend the following two hundred years trying to erase that first impression. The missionary martyrs of the

Yaquis peaceably, speaking to them in a friendly fashion and, more astonishing still, being similarly received by them.

After this foray into Sonora, he returned to Sinaloa, going as far south as Chametla. In the foothills behind Mazatlán – a town still very much in the future – he founded the Villa de San Sebastián de la Concordia and the mining towns of Copala and Pánuco, where he died in 1575.

northern territories far outnumber those of the south. In spite of such bitter hostility, the Jesuits, like the Franciscans in the northeast, ended by winning over the Indians. After founding their first mission in Culiacán in 1591, they founded others throughout western Chihuahua, Sinaloa, Sonora, Arizona, New Mexico and, a hundred years later, the Baja California peninsula.

The first expedition to venture inland left San Blas in 1678. A singularly gifted and purposeful Italian Jesuit by the name of Chini – remembered in Mexico as Father Kino – accompanied the expedition as Royal Cartographer. Though he was later immensely successful as an explorer and colonizer of Sonora and Arizona, Baja California utterly defeated him. A skirmish with the Indians

in La Paz and the disappearance of a soldier discouraged further exploration. Given the miserliness of the land and the abject condition of the natives, the early Jesuit missions in Baja California may perhaps be the only ones in the world to which no selfish purpose can be imputed.

TODAY

The trans–peninsular highway traverses the Baja California desert between the touristic poles of the peninsula: in the north the honky–tonky Tijuana, across the border from San Diego; and in the south, the luxurious seclusion of clubs and resort hotels of Cabo San Lucas and other nearby coves, capes, and islands. This southern tourist strip is

*Sonora. Alamos. Roof garden with view of
church, tower and cupolas.*

*Opposite page: Hacienda on the outskirts of
Alamos with ruins and a view of mountains.*

the rich man's Baja – as opposed to Tijuana, which defies description. Until the 1990's the frequenters of these posh resorts were neither tourists nor even travelers in the accepted sense of the word. They were generally well-heeled sportsmen to whom the trans-peninsular highway means nothing since they habitually flew their own planes or sailed their own boats to whichever destination they chose.

Across the Gulf of California – or Sea of Cortés – Sonora and Sinaloa have taken an entirely different tack. Their tourism is of the modern nomadic sort, with endless trailer caravans and crowded trailer parks. Mazatlán, straight across the Gulf of California from Cabos, is one of their big stops. Tourism is more important to Mazatlán than to any other town in these two big agricultural states – except perhaps the beautiful colonial city of Alamos in Sonora – and the local authorities have not allowed the old town to rot.

Mazatlán's charm resides in the stylistic consistency of the houses along its waterfront and downtown city blocks, all built in the tropical neoclassical style of tall iron-grilled windows and giant *zaguanes* (coach doors) topped by substantial cornices opening into the luminous interiors of airy corridors and high ceilings with fretted borders. This constitutes an architectural portrait of the substantial German, Spanish, and French merchant influx after Mexico's independence from Spain in 1821. Of the better known beach resorts, only Mazatlán fully represents this architecture.

Despite the restoration of the historic area, including a nineteenth-century opera house, parts of Mazatlán still reveal a town whose charm has been partially destroyed by the stranglehold of a few powerful landlords. The jungle of ficus roots lurking underground, sprouting out of every crack in the sidewalk and waiting to take over, has invaded the roofless shells of tall-windowed row houses. Strangler figs buttress their walls against hurricanes, their aerial roots dropping from branches to practice their Gaudí arabesques on the crumbling walls and cornices, following nature's obligation to imitate art.

HEADS OR TAILS, EAGLE OR SUN

In Mexico when you flip a coin you do not say "Heads or tails" but "*Aguila o sol*" – eagle or sun – the two sides of all our old coins. The eagle was the Aztec glyph for the sun, but it was also the devourer of human hearts that decorates our national emblem, and without which the sun would not rise for the Aztecs. Does it mean anything that the sun has disappeared from the modern Mexican coins but not the eagle?

In Sonora and Sinaloa we can see the flipping of the coin. Arbitrarily split up into two separate states in 1830, their economic activity – farming, fishing, cattle and poultry raising – and especially their technical approach to it, reveals the underlying unity of the region and the people. From Culiacán to Hermosillo a series of irrigation systems has made this northwestern corner of Mexico a farming emporium of prime impor-

Baja California.
Above: Mission of
San Ignacio.

Right: a typical
landscape.

Hacienda del mar,
one of the many
new resorts of
Los Cabos built
as a small town
showing a typical
palapa above
the pool.

Opposite page: Baja
California. View
with Biznaga cactus
in the foreground.

Photographic credits:

Bob Schalkwijk pages: 17, 22, 23, 48, 75, 104, 106, 108, 109, 110, 111, 119, 121, 122, 124, 124, 127, 128, 129, 130, 131, 132, 134, 135, 139, 139, 140, 140, 146, 148, 150, 159, 164, 172, 173, 174, 183, 184, 190, 191, 192, 193, 196, 202, 203, 204, 204, 205.

Horacio Hernandez pages: 27, 64, 67, 67, 102, 103, 107, 112, 168, 171, 208.

Francesco Venturi pages: 72, 80, 81, 82, 83, 83, 84, 85, 85, 86, 87, 88, 89.

All other photographs are by **Nicolas Sapieha**.